KWAME
NKRUMAH

KWAME NKRUMAH

by Yuri Smertin

INTERNATIONAL PUBLISHERS, New York

© 1987, Progress Publishers, Moscow

© U.S. edition, 1987
International Publishers Co., Inc.

Manufactured in the United States of America

Library of Congress Cataloging-in-Publication Data

Smertin, Yuri.
   Kwame Nkrumah.

   Includes index.
   1. Nkrumah, Kwame, 1909–1972. 2. Ghana – Presidents –
Biography. I. Title.
DT512.3.N57S6413   1987   966.7'05'0924[B]   87-2669
ISBN 0-7178-0655-3 (pbk.)

CONTENTS

Introduction

This book tells the story of the life and work of the former President of Ghana, Kwame Nkrumah. In our rapidly changing world each decade has its own political horizon, its own system of values, its own experiences. That is why it is at times difficult to evaluate the actions of a political leader who has passed from the scene.

But Kwame Nkrumah occupies a special place in the history of the African continent's liberation struggle, above all because he proved to be one of the most perspicacious leaders in Africa. He was among the first to realize that the revolution in Africa was and is part of the global anti-imperialist movement.

Kwame Nkrumah's political biography is complex and contradictory. During his lifetime, monuments were erected in Ghana in his honor and then torn down; after his death they were put up once more. The "Father of the Nation," as Nkrumah was called in Ghana, died in exile but his remains were brought home and buried with the greatest of honors. Nkrumah has been called and is still called a "Communist," "nationalist," "tyrant," "romantic," "dictator," "idealist," "pragmatist," etc. All of these terms suffer either from onesidedness or from bias and are incapable of defining as complex a politician as Kwame Nkrumah.

Many years have passed since a reactionary coup in Ghana deposed Nkrumah but interest in him has not abated in that time. Political groups in a variety of ideological camps strive to find a source of inspiration in the former President's extensive theoretical legacy and the facts of his life. African revolutionists and American Black nationalists, pseudo-leftist elements, bourgeois scholars and Marxist social scientists all draw on his works. Nkrumah's ideas have become the object of a fierce ideological struggle between the forces of reaction and progress, between those who speak out in favor of the African continent's socialist future and advocates of its capitalist evolution.

The national liberation of the peoples of Africa occurred in an age primarily characterized by the process of revolutionary transition from capitalism to socialism. For this reason national liberation revolutions frequently became anti-imperialist and even anti-capitalist and in a number of African countries this development resulted in the coming to power of progressive, patriotic forces who proclaimed socialism to be their goal. One of the first countries to step onto the path of non-capitalist development was Ghana, under the leadership of Kwame Nkrumah.

The majority of African countries won political independence in the late 1950s and early 1960s. At this time of the general surge in anti-imperialist feeling in Africa, theories arose that denied the existence of capitalist conflicts in African countries and called for the specific features of African society to be taken into account when choosing socialism as a goal. One who held this point of view was Kwame Nkrumah, who led the struggle for progressive socio-economic reforms in his country. He declared that the continent's future was bound up with socialism.

However, the theories concerning a "national type" of socialism, which presupposed the absence of class contradictions in African countries, came to hinder the progressive transformation of society. Reactionary coups occurred in some countries, including Ghana.

The role of the individual in history has been discussed in the classics of Marxism-Leninism. In his *Thesis on Feuerbach* Marx wrote, "But the essence of man is no abstraction inherent in each single individual. In its reality it is the ensemble of the social relations."[1]

In Marxist-Leninist theory, objective processes play the decisive role in society's evolution. Nevertheless the individual has never been considered a passive force. Lenin wrote, "... the idea of historical necessity does not in the least undermine the role of the individual in history; all history is made up of the actions of individuals, who are undoubtedly active figures. The real question that arises in appraising the social activity of an individual is: what conditions ensure the success of his actions, what guarantee is there that these actions will not remain an isolated act lost in a welter of contrary acts?"[2]

No matter how great an individual's political significance, one can neither suspend nor reverse the objective historical process. He or she can, however, influence this process, accelerating it or temporarily slowing

[1]Marx/Engels *Collected Works* [*CW*] 5:p.4.
[2]V. I. Lenin, *CW 1:* 159.

it down. The recognition a political leader gains is determined by the accuracy with which he sizes up any situation either within the country or beyond its borders, by the ability to work out the right strategy and tactics for struggle and by links with the masses.

In the present historical age, the most farsighted and realistic African leaders have consciously made a choice in favor of socialism. Kwame Nkrumah declared that African states could solve their problems only if they let themselves be guided by a powerful and creative doctrine – scientific socialism. Marxist-Leninist theory had an enormous influence on Nkrumah's world outlook.

KWAME
NKRUMAH

I.The Early Years

Nkrumah loved sunsets and tried never to miss those brief, ever exciting minutes. Today the sunset seemed particularly beautiful. As it sank into the ocean the crimson sun was reflected by a myriad of patches of light in the line of surf. No sooner had the upper edge of the sun vanished than the entire horizon was painted in glowing colors – orange, red and purple. The palms along the shore suddenly became visible, their crowns making fantastic shapes against the blazing sky. But soon the colors faded and then were extinguished altogether. Only a narrow red band remained a few minutes longer at the spot where the fiery disc had disappeared.

Darkness enveloped the study. Nkrumah turned on the lights and wearily sat down at his large desk. He needed to record the main events of the past few days, days which would become part of his country's history forever. The day before yesterday, on September 18, 1956, it had been learned that Britain had finally announced the date on which the independence of the Gold Coast would be declared – March 6, 1957. Yesterday he had passed this long-awaited news on to the Legislative Assembly and this evening he had made the announcement over the radio. His free country would bear the proud name Ghana. That had been the name of a rich and powerful medieval state established by the peoples of West Africa.

A few sheets of paper covered with neat handwriting lay in a thick folder labelled "autobiography." Nkrumah had been working on it by fits and starts for many months now. No, it was not the desire to tell the world about his life that had made him put pen to paper. He wanted to record the history of the anti-colonial struggle waged by the people of the Gold Coast, the struggle to which he had devoted his life. The autobiography of Jawaharlal Nehru – the leader of one of the first Asian countries to be liberated from British colonial rule – had made a big impression on Nkrumah. His country was to become the first state in Tropical Africa to wrench itself free from the colonial system.

1

"As a ship that has been freshly launched, we face the hazards of the high seas alone. We must rely on our own men, on the captain and on his navigation. And, as I proudly stand on the bridge of that lone vessel as she confidently sets sail, I raise a hand to shade my eyes from the glaring African sun and scan the horizon. There is so much more beyond,"[1] wrote Nkrumah. The book was finished. And then again, not quite. Turning to the first page he wrote in big letters, "To my mother." At that moment in his mind's eye he saw his mother – young, smiling, serene and resolute – the way she was when he was a child.

Kwame Nkrumah was born in September 1909 in the tiny village of Nkroful in the southwestern part of what is now Ghana, the area where the Nzima people of the Akan tribe lived. Here as everywhere the birth of a child is a joyous event. Careful preparations for his arrival are made not only by the future mother and father but by his numerous relatives as well. However, the birth of the young Nyanibah's first child was clouded by other events. For several days prior to the birth Nkrumah's relatives had been mourning the death of his father's mother, a respected individual in the village. Nevertheless, the newborn was soon the center of attention. Two weeks later, when according to custom the time had come to choose a name for the child, the father invited the family's friends and relatives to the ceremony and opened a bottle of wine he had set aside for this occasion. The oldest person present spilled a little of the wine on the earthen floor of the hut. Summoning the ancestral spirits and deities who protected the family, he put the child in their care. The remaining wine was drunk to the health of the new member of the Anona clan from which his mother was descended. According to tradition the child belonged to his mother's family. But the father alone had the right to choose the child's name. The Akans attach great significance to the day of the week on which an infant comes into the world and each day corresponds to a specific name. As the boy had been born on a Saturday he was named Kwame.

Kwame was his mother's only child; even so, the family was fairly large. His father had several wives and the little boy's main playmates were his numerous half-brothers. The number of wives a man in Tropical Africa had was indicative of his social status. Nkrumah's father was a petty artisan. He made bracelets, earrings and rings out of gold and peddled his wares in the surrounding towns and villages. His mother, like many other women, worked in the fields and sold produce at the local market.

---

[1]Kwame Nkrumah, *Ghana: The Autobiography of Kwame Nkrumah,* Thomas Nelson & Sons, Edinburgh, 1957, p. 288.

In 1900 the British took the last step towards complete annexation of the Gold Coast and included it among their "crown" possessions. Nevertheless, life in Nkrumah's native village went unchanged. Mornings began as they had for hundreds of years with the sound of staccato pounding coming from all directions. The women were mashing cassavas in large wooden mortars with long pestles. The mashed cassavas were used to make a traditional dish called fou-fou which was heated over charcoal. After breakfast the women swept the floor of their huts and the area around them and then either set off for the stream to do laundry or, together with their husbands and grown children, shouldered their hoes and went to work in the fields.

When Kwame was about three years old his father, who worked at a jeweller's in the small town of Half Assini at the time, brought Nyanibah and their son to live with him. Life in their new home did not differ much from the familiar village round. The wives in the family took turns cooking, working in the fields and going to the market to sell all kinds of things: vegetables, fruit, eggs, meat, fish, etc. The money the women made was theirs to keep and gave them a degree of material independence. Kwame's father was usually either at the jewellers' or on sales trips. Like other children Kwame was left to his own devices all day. In the evening his mother would take a break from the endless housework, seat the little boy at her side and tell him stories about the Akan tribe which had been handed down from generation to generation. They were peopled by witches, apparitions, ghosts, sorcerers, wronged women, successful merchants and, naturally, noble heroes. At these moments the boundaries between fantasy and reality, between the imagined and that which actually exists disappeared. Good usually triumphed in the end. Through his mother's stories Kwame absorbed the traditions of his people and comprehended their wisdom, moral code and the way in which they conceptualized the world. Nkrumah loved his mother dearly. She was not only a kind instructor to him but also his best friend. This profound feeling remained with him throughout his life. According to people who were close to him, many years later when he was head of state he said, "My mother is a tower of strength to me. . . . I have never cared for any woman as much as I have cared for her. We are both alike in one thing – we seem to draw strength from each other. In the same way I feel better for seeing her, she gets better if she is ill and I visit her."[1]

[1] Genoveva Marais, *Kwame Nkrumah: As I Knew Him,* Janay Publishing Company, Chichester, 1972, p. 85.

Nkrumah's mother could neither read nor write; nor could his father, for that matter. Nevertheless, it was she who insisted that Kwame should have an education. The school where he was sent was run by Catholic missionaries and the instructors were Europeans. Nkrumah was not used to school with its strict discipline and rigid daily routine and he made a firm decision to drop out. His mother, however, had different ideas. The first weeks she took him by the hand, walked to school with him and sat him on his bench. Nkrumah had no choice but to learn to love school. Promoting this to no small degree was the teacher's cane – children who were careless about their lessons frequently got a taste of it. All of the grades were in one room and the teacher taught English, arithmetic and geography to each in turn. Religion was considered the main subject. The young Nkrumah took his studies of the Holy Scriptures very seriously, served as an altar boy and loved to discuss religion with his teacher. He was baptized in the Roman Catholic Church and received the christian name Francis.

Because he finished his eight years of schooling near the top of his class, Nkrumah was given a job as a pupil-teacher at one of the primary schools in Half Assini. Now he was the one who was teaching fidgety boys but, in contrast to the teachers he had had, he taught by conviction rather than by the cane. The teenager's pedagogical gifts came to the attention of the school's administrators and they recommended him for further study in Accra.

In 1927 Kwame Nkrumah entered the Accra Training College. In those days Accra was an insignificant colonial capital with a population of around 50,000. Nevertheless, it made a big impression on the boy from the provinces. Frenziedly honking cars and buses rushed about the streets. Crowds of people speaking loudly in a variety of tongues filled the pavements. Here, the bright clothes of the coastal dwellers, people from Ashanti and the Northern Territories, the Hausa from neighbouring Nigeria, Syrians, Lebanese and Greeks mingled, creating a riot of color. Downtown the streets were "occupied" by African women who advertised the wares they had spread out on the pavement – cola nuts, fish, perfume, oranges, razor blades, medicines and much, much more. Here the women sold fried fish, plantain and a rice and meat dish prepared over oil stoves. Shops owned by foreign companies and large buildings containing the offices of the British lined the streets. The private residences of the British colonial officials were situated in an area far from the center of town. It was a quiet place and rarely did an African go there if he did not have specific business to attend to. Only the fringes of the city reminded Nkrumah of home. The houses bore a greater resemblance to huts with their gardens and fields of cassava and maize. Chickens darted about and black goats stamped their hooves in the dusty yards.

The first year in Accra was not an easy one for Nkrumah. He was frequently homesick for Half Assini where his mother was. In 1927 his father died of blood poisoning and, for all intents and purposes, the family broke up. His mother left Half Assini and, in keeping with tradition, went to live with the brother of her deceased husband.

The person who managed to pull Nkrumah out of his depression and later had a great influence on the molding of his world outlook was an African teacher, Kwegyir Aggrey. Before coming to the Gold Coast he had studied for many years in the United States. There he had worked on his doctoral dissertation and was appointed to be one of the directors of the Prince of Wales' College which had just opened in Achimota, not far from Accra; it was the first institution of higher learning in the colony.

The man with the kindly, slightly ironic gaze who always wore European clothes was one of the first Africans to speak out against the existing educational system under which schoolchildren were taught British history and British geography from A to Z, sang British songs (the particular favorite of teachers was "Rule Britannia") and knew nothing of the history, traditions and culture of their own peoples. Nkrumah's mentor maintained that there would come a day when the young Africa would wake up and make its existence known. But, Kwegyir Aggrey believed, harmonious cooperation between Blacks and whites was necessary if this great goal was to be achieved.

In his autobiography Kwame Nkrumah declared that even at that time he could not accept this idea. He wrote, " . . . such harmony can only exist when the black race is treated as equal to the white race; . . . only a free and independent people – a people with a government of their own – can claim equality, racial or otherwise, with another people."[1] Thanks to Aggrey, Nkrumah noted, a sense of national pride was first awakened in him. Nkrumah's friendship with this man who so captured his imagination lasted less than a year. For his holidays Aggrey went to the USA and from there came the news of his sudden death.

In 1928 the Accra Training College was moved to Achimota and made part of the Prince of Wales' College. The staff included both Europeans and Africans. Most of the members of Kwame Nkrumah's new class had

[1]*Ghana*, p. 14.

parents who belonged to the local population's privileged sectors: their fathers were chiefs, merchants or clerks in the colonial administration. In contrast to Nkrumah they had finished secondary school and he tried to fill in the gaps in his education (Latin and higher mathematics in particular) by associating with them.

Nkrumah was an enthusiast by nature. It was hard for him to tear himself away from whatever he was busy with and for that reason he was not considered a well-disciplined student. His interests were varied. The religious ardor of his teens had cooled somewhat. Classes in history, psychology, public speaking and other subjects began to take up most of 'his time. In addition to his studies he went in for sports and amateur theatricals· he ran for the college in the 100- and 200-yard dashes and played the lead in "Kofi Goes Abroad." The main point of the play was to show the importance the knowledge that young men like Kofi gained in England in the field of medicine had for the people of the Gold Coast.

The Prince of Wales' College was at that time a typical colonial educational establishment which inculcated pro-British sentiments in its students. Many years later, Nkrumah described the situation that had prevailed at the college: "...curriculum, discipline and sports were as close imitations as possible of those operating in English public schools. The object was to train up a western oriented political elite committed to the attitudes and ideologies of capitalism and bourgeois society."[1] Naturally, at the time he was unable to evaluate the education he was receiving in such categorical terms. Nevertheless, Kwame Nkrumah was already coming to the realization that the colonial regime was unlawful and had no future. The usual career of an African intellectual, which promised to provide him with a reasonable living, did not suit the young Nkrumah. Upon graduating from the Prince of Wales' College in 1930 he made a firm decision to go into education and, if the opportunity arose, to continue his studies abroad.

Nkrumah's career in teaching began at the Roman Catholic junior school in Elmina. The sight of the five- and six-year-old boys who were his charges, full of irrepressible energy, reminded him of his first years at the school in Half Assini and he did his best to be kind and attentive to his pupils, using the subject matter to capture and hold their attention. Basil Davidson's biography of Nkrumah quotes a former British school inspector who once sat in on a lesson given by the young teacher. "I have never

---

[1]Kwame Nkrumah, *Class Struggle in Africa,* International Publishers, New York, 1970, pp. 36-37.

forgotten our meeting . . . since I was suddenly made aware that here was no ordinary teacher. Despite a frieze of noisy spectators at the open windows, the pupils reacted to his calm, dignified and 'magnetic' manner wholeheartedly. It was an unforgettable inspectorial experience."[1]

Kwame Nkrumah had an abiding interest in his country's past. On a sandbar in Elmina there rose an old fortress, made of white stone and surrounded by palms, which had been built by the Portuguese. For Nkrumah that fortress was the embodiment of the most dismal pages in the history of the Gold Coast.

The first Portuguese ships appeared off the Gold Coast in 1471. It acquired the name Gold Coast later when the Portuguese found deposits of gold there. The peaceable indigenous population made its living by tilling the soil and fishing. The Portuguese went there as conquerors and decided to settle down for a long stay. They shipped in blocks of stone from Portugal and made a gloomy fortress out of them. It was to be the bastion that would guard the gold mines. They named the fortress Elmina which means "the mine." Soon, however, the Europeans' main source of income came to be a "live commodity" – Black slaves. From among the Africans who had been captured in the inland regions of the Gold Coast, the Portuguese chose the strongest and healthiest. The rest they killed. The fortress became a slave market. Here the slaves were branded and then driven along a narrow underground passageway to the shore and the slaver that would take them to Europe or the New World. In the 17th century the Portuguese were forced out of the Gold Coast by the Dutch who were in the slave trade on an even larger scale. Every time he went to the fortress Kwame Nkrumah could almost hear his distant ancestors' groans and cries of despair. It seemed to him that these wretches were appealing to him to wreak vengeance for the terrible wrong that had been done them.

After one year in Elmina, Nkrumah was named headmaster of the Roman Catholic junior school in Aksima. The region was populated by members of his own tribe and Nkrumah organised a Nzima literary society. There he met the person who was to become his first political mentor. His name was Samuel R. Wood. At that time he was Secretary of the National Congress of British West Africa. This organization, which had come into being in 1920s, brought together civic leaders from four

---

[1]Basil Davidson, *Black Star: A View of the Life and Times of Kwame Nkrumah,* Allen Lane, London, 1973, pp. 23-24.

British colonies – the Gold Coast, Nigeria, Sierra Leone and Gambia. The goal of the organization was to gain some measure of self-government for the four countries through a series of gradual reforms within the framework of the colonial regime. In the history textbooks used in colonial schools and colleges Africans were seen as the object of the historical process while the subject was the "metropolitan country" and the "white world". The history of Nkrumah's country was rendered as the history of the governors and their administrations. From Wood, Nkrumah learned of the political and cultural life of the West Africans. Their talks were frequent and long. The ideas of such ideologists of African nationalism as the Sierra Leonean James A. B. Horton, the well-known African scholar Edward W. Blyden, and his pupil and follower from the Gold Coast, Joseph Casely-Hayford, had a great impact on Nkrumah.

Back in the 1860s James A. B. Horton had put forward the idea of granting all of West Africa independence. In his book *West African Countries and Peoples,* he asserted the right of Africans to self-government and criticized those British "social anthropologists" who had created the "theory" that the Negro race was mentally inferior. Edward Blyden, one of the first ideologists of pan-Africanism, substantiated his notion of the African peoples' common destiny in numerous scholarly works. At the end of the 19th century he put forward the concept of the distinctiveness of the "African Personality" and "spiritual decolonization." This concept was taken up by many of the ideologists of African nationalism. In 1913 Casely-Hayford launched a campaign to establish a West African federation. "One touch of nature has made all West Africa kin," he wrote. "The common danger to our ancestral lands has made us one – one in danger, one in safety. United we stand, divided we fall . . . "[1] He assigned educated African youth a fundamental role in this movement. It was to them he addressed this appeal: "We want thinkers, thinkers of great thoughts. We want leaders, born leaders of men."[2]

The views of the first African nationalists had a great impact on the young Nkrumah's still unformed world outlook. He shared their views for the most part. But Nkrumah objected to the opinion expressed by the leaders of the National Congress of British West Africa that political indepen-

---

[1]Quoted in: *Ideologies of Liberation in Black Africa,* 1856-1970. Documents on modern African political thought from colonial times to the present, ed. by J. Ayo Langley, Rex Collings, London, 1979, p. 208.

[2]Ibid., p. 209.

dence for the peoples of Africa would be feasible only after a lengthy period of peaceful cooperation with the white colonialists. This was thought to be essential if experience in governing was to be acquired and broad sections of the African population were to become educated. Nkrumah believed that one had to start with political action. Events in the Gold Coast upheld Nkrumah's views.

The world economic crisis of the 1930s, which had dealt a severe blow to the capitalist countries, also had serious consequences for their colonies. The catastrophic drop in the foreign demand for cacao beans – the Gold Coast's principal source of revenue – led to a sharp deterioration in the already disastrous situation of the common people. In an attempt to shift the full burden of their economic difficulties onto the shoulders of working men and women the British colonial authorities cut working people's wages and carried out mass dismissals at the country's few industrial enterprises. In the wake of these events the colony's population was considerably politicized: trade unions were formed and workers went on strike. The local African press and the numerous cultural and educational organizations run by Africans furthered the spread of anti-colonial sentiment. The birth of widespread political awareness in the Gold Coast dates from the 1930s.

Nnamdi Azikiwe, who later became the first President of independent Nigeria, came to the Gold Coast in 1934 after nine years of study in the United States and became the editor of *The African Morning Post*. In his passionately denunciatory articles and public statements he censured the existing colonial order: the restrictions on the Africans' right to express their opinions, and racial discrimination. He also criticized those Africans who belonged to the "elite" of colonial society and favored retaining the existing order, as they regarded it as the basis of their well-being. Azikiwe enjoyed enormous popularity, particularly among young people. In later years Nkrumah recalled that Azikiwe's articles had exerted a large influence on the formation of his national consciousness. For anti-colonial speeches and incitement to revolt, Azikiwe was sentenced to six months in prison. Some time later he was released and he returned to Nigeria.

At that time Nkrumah's sentiments were predominantly anti-colonial. However neither he nor, for that matter, the other African nationalists, could offer any clear alternatives to the existing order. Educated Africans still pinned their hopes on reforms aimed at altering the essence of colonialism. For many the United States of America represented the ideal of liberty and equality. African intellectuals based their judgment of the U.S. chiefly on the American constitution, which formally granted Blacks and whites equal rights. That is why Nkrumah decided to cross the ocean to continue his education even though inhabitants of the British colonies or rather – those lucky few who were given the opportunity – usually received their university education in England. At the close of 1934 he sent his application to Lincoln University – the first institution of higher learning for Black people in the United States – and received notice of his acceptance. Now his chief problem was money for the trip. A well-to-do relative in Nigeria came to his aid. Nkrumah returned from Lagos with one hundred pounds sterling and the confidence that his plans would come to fruition. All that remained to be done was to make the final preparations prior to departure and say goodbye to his mother.

It was a difficult parting. At first his mother could not understand why her son needed to go to a distant and mysterious land of white people now, when he had become a man of learning and had a good job. To teach at the Roman Catholic Junior School in Amissano was a great honor for any educated young man. Moreover, her son was fully entitled to become the chief of the Dadieso and Nsaeum tribes because her distinguished clan traced its ancestry back to the sister of the great Aduku Addaie who had brought the Nzima to this area. They talked the night away. The next morning Nyanibah made breakfast for her son and then accompanied him to the ford where a boat was waiting for him. "It cannot be helped . . . may God and your ancestors guide you,"[1] she said in parting.

[1] *Ghana*, p. 26.

II. American Universities

In those days the road to the United States lay through London where the American embassy issued visas to inhabitants of the British colonies. In August 1935 Kwame Nkrumah boarded a small steamer in Takoradi bound for Liverpool. The painful parting with his mother, loneliness and an inexplicable fear of the future threw Nkrumah into a state of despair. He spotted a slip of paper on his berth and, complaining of the poor cleaning job which had been done in his cabin, was about to throw it in the wastepaper basket when he realized that it was a telegram addressed to him: Azikiwe himself had thought it necessary to reassure the young African. "Goodbye. Remember to trust in God and yourself,"[1] it read. Nkrumah regained his composure. Recalling that Azikiwe had called on African youth to "go to the United States and . . . come back with the Golden Fleece,"[2] he thought of himself as Jason while the ancient steamer became the legendary Argo.

The trip was uneventful. At last the boat docked in Liverpool. With a beating heart Nkrumah stepped onto the shore of the land that beckoned to him and frightened him at the same time.

He journeyed to London, a city that impressed Nkrumah with its efficiency, crowded streets, colorful advertisements and endless succession of autos, double-decker buses and trams. The British capital was slowly recovering from the knockout blow the global economic crisis had dealt it, although in the country as a whole more than two million people were unemployed.

Nkrumah was already familiar with many of London's sights, having seen them in photographs and drawings. He easily found the Monument, the massive column slightly under seventy meters tall which had been

---

[1]*Ghana,* p. 26.
[2]Basil Davidson, *Black Star . . . ,* p. 29.

erected in memory of the Great Fire of 1666. The guidebooks promised
that anyone who mounted the more than three hundred steps to the
observation platform was in for an unforgettable experience. They spoke
the truth: the view of the British capital it afforded was impressive.
Immediately before him stretched the City, the business district with its
tall, modern office buildings. The heart of London beat visibly: streams of
people and cars flowed along the arterial streets fanning out from that
point. On the horizon the great bulk of St. Paul's Cathedral rose up. From
the other side of the Monument a majestic view of the top of Tower
Bridge opened up. To the left, the Tower itself could just be made out
through the haze. Pleasure boats slowly crept along the Thames. Automobile horns, the tooting of steamboats, the clank of the harbor and the
hollow rumble of the Tube merged and became a backdrop of sound
which enveloped this city of eight million. London led its life, a life little
understood by Nkrumah.

Kwame Nkrumah set off for Hyde Park and the famous Speaker's
Corner where, as he knew, anyone could get up and present his ideas.
After listening to a Catholic priest and a Protestant minister – who stood
on wooden stepladders not far from one another sluggishly proving that
theirs was the one true faith – Nkrumah felt somewhat disappointed.
Surely there were more important and pressing problems to discuss.

Those were troubled times. Menacing clouds of war had already gathered
over the world. The Nazi Wehrmacht was feverishly arming itself, setting
up the air force prohibited by the Treaty of Versailles. The Soviet Union
urged London and Paris not to reject the principle of collective security.
Ethiopia asked the League of Nations to take effective steps to prevent the
war Italy threatened her with, but in vain. The militaristic alliance between
Germany and Japan was taking shape. One day when he was walking
down Fleet Street, Nkrumah saw a headline whose meaning he did not
immediately grasp: "Mussolini Invades Ethiopia 3 October." The newspaper boys cried, "Italian tanks attack main road between Asmara and Addis
Ababa." Nkrumah was struck dumb. Ethiopia, the oldest independent
state in the Black Continent, was a symbol of liberty for African nationalists.
And now Italian fascism was trying to destroy that island of liberty with
the connivance of the Western "democracies." In his autobiography
Nkrumah wrote, "At that moment it was almost as if the whole of London
had suddenly declared war on me personally. For the next few minutes I
could do nothing but glare at each impassive face wondering if these
people could possibly realise the wickedness of colonialism, and praying

that the day might come when I could play my part in bringing about the downfall of such a system."[1]

At long last all the formalities were out of the way and Nkrumah set out across the Atlantic from Liverpool on a Cunard White Star Line steamship. The voyage was favored with good weather. Early one October morning the ship sailed into New York. The gigantic buildings rose like a mirage in the gray sky. There, on the starboard side, stood the famous statue of a woman holding a torch in one hand and gazing impassively out to sea. "Liberty," Nkrumah whispered. Here was the golden fleece for which he had crossed the ocean.

New York stunned and bewildered the young African. This city was not like Accra or Liverpool or London. Nkrumah felt as though he had wandered on stage in the middle of a revue. Only in Harlem, where he stayed for two days with an acquaintance from Sierra Leone, did Nkrumah manage to regain at least part of his equilibrium. Harlem did not have the same dressed-up crowds, the continuous stream of honking cars, the glittering shop windows. Here he did not stand out because of the color of his skin, the way he dressed or the amount of money in his billfold.

Classes had begun two months before at Lincoln. Nkrumah passed his exams and caught up with his classmates. The school, founded in the early 1850s, was small. The student body consisted chiefly of American Black students but there were some Africans as well. Nkrumah even ran into a young man from Accra, Ako Adjei, who subsequently became a good friend. Nnamdi Azikiwe, too, had once studied here. Nkrumah eagerly absorbed the new knowledge that was offered him and spent long hours in the library. Having set his sights on a career in politics, he mastered the art of public speaking and won a gold medal at a college speech contest.

Nkrumah's abilities were noticed. One day an upperclassman whom he barely knew approached him with an offer to join the Phi Beta Sigma fraternity. Receiving Nkrumah's word that he would keep the conversation a secret, the upperclassman gave the freshman the instructions for pledges. They were long and confusing and contained a vow of loyalty to the fraternity whose motto was "Culture for Service and Service for Humanity". The instruction's main message was that members should help one another and get acquainted at all times and everywhere with people who might be of interest to the fraternity. This was followed by a

[1]*Ghana,* p. 27.

list of persons famous in the worlds of business, culture, science and religion who had joined Phi Beta Sigma in college and retained their fraternity membership.

Student fraternities are a common phenomenon in U.S. universities. At the time Nkrumah attended Lincoln University, this student elite occupied all of the key posts in university organizations. More importantly, its members kept in contact after graduation.

Kwame Nkrumah went through what was to him a degrading initiation and became a full member of Phi Beta Sigma. He was to retain an unpleasant aftertaste as well as a special tie pin as mementos of this chapter in his life. Unfortunately, helping one's fellow fraternity members, discussed a great deal in the instructions, did not imply financial assistance for needy brothers. Even by living as modestly as possible Nkrumah could not make ends meet on his scholarship. Thus he was always on the lookout for ways to earn extra money. He had a part-time job in the university library and wrote sociology and economics papers for less-than-diligent students, charging a dollar a paper. And still he could not make ends meet.

During his summer holidays Nkrumah went to New York and, together with his friend from Sierra Leone, started a business, his first. Early in the morning they would buy fish at the market where prices were low and then sell it in the streets in the afternoon for a profit. That is what his mother and the other women venders had always done in the Gold Coast. In vain did they press the fish on passersby. Their engaging smiles met only indifference. Clearly, Nkrumah decided, other economic laws are at work here. In two weeks their enterprise was bankrupt. The ex-partners quarrelled and Nkrumah was forced to find a new place to live and some sort of job.

While he found a small room in Harlem with relative ease – he had to spend only one night in the subway – his search for a summer job seemed completely hopeless.

The United States had still not recovered from the economic crisis. The newspapers called this period the Great Depression. Most of Nkrumah's Harlem neighbors had despaired of finding any kind of work at all. Seeing people spend their days digging through garbage cans in search of table scraps, Nkrumah viewed his immediate future with pessimism. On the advice of friends he decided to go to Philadelphia.

Fate smiled on him. Although the employment situation there was no better, he managed to get a job as a dishwasher on a ship which plied between New York and the Mexican city of Veracruz. Suffocating in the steam as he scrubbed the greasy pots and pans, Nkrumah was almost happy. Here he did not have to worry where his next meal was coming from and he had been promised a decent paycheck at the end of the voyage. The diligence of the beginner was noticed and he received a promotion. Now he was entrusted with washing plates. This was followed by an even more dizzying rise up the "job ladder." Nkrumah became a waiter and then a messenger. That was as high as a Black member of the ship's crew could go. Rich passengers occasionally gave him good tips, and evenings – when he counted his savings – in his mind Nkrumah spent it on books.

Nkrumah made friends with his fellow crew members. Honesty, a straightforward manner and a sense of fellowship are valued on all seas and oceans equally. And Nkrumah liked the maritime life, so far removed from the stiff atmosphere pervading the halls of the university. Every summer until 1939, when World War II broke out, he found work on seagoing vessels.

The university years flew by. In 1939 Kwame Nkrumah graduated from Lincoln University with a Bachelor's degree in economics and sociology. The university yearbook named him the "most interesting" member of the graduating class. He had to forget his dreams of entering the Columbia University School of Journalism: he just did not have the money for that. Instead, he accepted an invitation to remain at the university and become a philosophy assistant. The new job required that he expand his knowledge of philosophy and thus Nkrumah discovered the astounding world of abstract ideas, logical categories and laws. He avidly absorbed all that was new to him, all that had been unfamiliar to him before or about which he had entertained highly superficial ideas. He devoted all his free time to studying Descartes, Freud and subsequently Kant, Nietzsche, Hegel, Schopenhauer and Spinoza. He read Ibsen and Tolstoy with great interest.

In that same year, 1939, Nkrumah was accepted by the Lincoln Theological Seminary. He had little interest in the various trends within Christianity and did not see anything strange in the fact that he, a professed Catholic, should be studying Presbyterian theology. On Sundays Nkrumah frequently delivered sermons in Black churches. Nkrumah began studying philosophy and education at Pennsylvania University. In 1942 he was awarded two degrees – a Bachelor's in theology and a Master's in education. The following year he defended his thesis in philosophy. After passing his doctoral exams Nkrumah set to work on his dissertation. Financially his situation was as precarious as ever. In order to at least get by he took a job as a counter in the Sun Shipbuilding Yard in Chester. From midnight to 8 a.m. Nkrumah worked at the harbor. Then, after resting a bit, he plunged back into the world of philosophical problems, so far removed from real life. This kind of exhausting schedule sapped Nkrumah's health. He contracted pneumonia and was taken to the hospital in serious condition. His dissertation had to be put aside for a while.

Although he was extremely busy, Nkrumah devoted a good deal of time to the study of Africa's history and culture. He helped set up the African Studies Section at the University of Pennsylvania. At the university library he gathered a great deal of valuable information on the Fanti language and on the beliefs and customs of the Akan. Nkrumah attempted to answer for himself a question that concerned those Africans who came in direct contact with Western civilization: how could the traditional culture of Africa and European culture be correlated? Nkrumah came to the conclusion that the two cultures must be synthesized. A new culture would spring from this synthesis – the culture of a free Africa. In 1943 he wrote, "The problem now is how to educate and then initiate the African into modern life without uprooting him from his home and tribal life."[1] Nkrumah sharply criticized those Africans who were cut off from their traditions.

Kwame Nkrumah was particularly interested in the life of Black people in the United States. One Presbyterian congregation commissioned him to conduct a survey of Black families. In Philadelphia alone he visited the homes of more than 600 Black Americans. Nkrumah no longer had any illusions about the conditions under which Blacks lived; nevertheless, what he saw shocked him. Later he commented: "the work...was certainly an eye-opener to the racial problem in the United States..."[2] Black people were the most deprived group in the "equal opportunity society," occupying the lowest rung on the social ladder. They were the first to fall victim to unemployment. Their level of education was extremely low. Hardest hit were young people who were without means of earning a living. The overwhelming majority lived in ghettos. At that time the number of Black workers who were moving to the industrial north from the South in search of work was growing. Twenty years later Martin Luther King used these words to describe the plight of the Black popula-

---

[1]Imanuel Geiss, *The Pan-African Movement,* Africana Publishing Co., New York, 1974, p. 373.

[2]*Ghana,* p. 42.

tion in the U.S.: "To be a Negro in America is often to hope against hope ... This is truly an island of poverty in the midst of an ocean of plenty."[1]

After seeing how Black Americans lived, Nkrumah came to the conclusion that the policies the U.S. government pursued in relation to them had a great deal in common with the colonial policies pursued by European powers. He formed an interest in two of the most important Black leaders of that time, W. E. B. Du Bois and Marcus Garvey.

A talented social commentator and world-famous scholar, Du Bois consistently fought for the rights of Black people in the United States. In 1905 he founded the Niagara Movement, an organization which fought for the civil rights of Black Americans. For twenty years Du Bois was the publisher and editor of *Crisis,* a magazine with a large Black readership. This magazine popularized the ideas of his organization and told the world of the plight of the outcast Black citizens. The nation's acute racial problem came to the attention of broad sections of the public. In 1910 the National Association for the Advancement of Colored People (NAACP) was founded. Most of the members of the Niagara Movement joined the new organization which brought together progressively oriented white intellectuals, civic activists, philanthropists and Blacks who were ready to fight for their liberation. Du Bois became one of the leaders of the new organization and was in large part responsible for its democratization and radicalization. His criticism of the capitalist colonial system was largely based on Marxist tenets. In 1961 Du Bois joined the Communist Party, USA.

Du Bois visited the Soviet Union in 1926 and 1936; In the United States, he ardently proclaimed the achievements of the young socialist country. W. E. B. Du Bois is famous not only as an advocate of civil rights. His name is also linked with the founding of the pan-African movement. It was this aspect of Du Bois's activities which most interested Nkrumah.

Pan-Africanism first arose in the U.S. as a political movement at the end of the 19th century. The keynote of pan-Africanism was the common destiny that bound together the African peoples, their solidarity in the fight against racism and colonialism regardless of where they lived – in Africa, the United States or the West Indies. The movement emerged in reaction to the brutal racist terror to which American Negroes were

---

[1]Martin Luther King, Jr., *Where Do We Go from Here: Chaos or Community?,* Harper & Row Publishers, New York, 1967, p. 113.

subjected and the colonial enslavement of African peoples. Up until the end of the Second World War, the U.S. was the biggest forum for pan-African ideas because in Africa any political activity was suppressed by the colonialists. Nevertheless the ideas of pan-African nationalism were also popular on the African continent, particularly in the west, among intellec- tuals who were inspired by the struggle Black Americans were waging. At Du Bois's initiative three pan-African congresses were held – in 1919, 1921 and 1923. In order to direct the attention of the world public to the plight of the indigenous population of the African colonies, the congresses were held in Paris, Brussels and Lisbon, the capitals of three colonial powers. The Pan-Africanists did not have a common goal nor was their class make-up homogeneous. Du Bois led the more radical, anti-imperialist wing. Meeting Du Bois and becoming acquainted with his ideas played an important part in the formation of the young Nkrumah's views.

At the time Du Bois was organizing the NAACP there arose a second Black movement, the Back to Africa movement, headed by the famous Black leader of the 1920s, Marcus Garvey. He called on Black Americans to leave the United States, where they were the victims of poverty and racism, and go to Africa which would become the continent of liberty for Black people everywhere. In making his appeal Garvey ignored the fact that Africa was under the yoke of colonialism. Garvey quickly set up the Universal Negro Improvement Association, a mass organization that claimed hundreds of thousands of members. In order to bring his ideas to fruition he founded a steamship company, the Black Star Line. Garvey favored the economic independence of Blacks from whites. He set up factories and companies that employed Black labor exclusively. However, Garvey was soon ruined when he became entangled in a web of financial difficulties. Nkrumah never had a chance to meet Garvey, although it was one of his dreams. Frightened by Garvey's popularity, the U.S. authorities fabricated a charge – unlawful use of the U.S. mails – and sentenced him to prison. Two years later he was released and deported to his native island of Jamaica.

Garvey proclaimed the "purity of the Black race", thereby awakening in Black people a sense of ethnic self-awareness and pride in their past, overcoming the feeling that the Negro race was inferior which had been instilled in them for centuries. That is why Garveyism attracted not only the oppressed masses of Black Americans but Africans as well. Marcus Garvey made a deep impression on Nkrumah, who was getting ready to pursue a career in politics. "I think that of all the literature that I studied," he later wrote, "the book that did more than any other to fire my enthusiasm was *Philosophy and Opinions of Marcus Garvey*, published in 1923."[1] Henceforth Nkrumah would make extensive use of Garvey's call for the creation of the United States of Africa. The state shipping company in independent Ghana was named the Black Star Line. Nkrumah did not, however, believe in the "purity of the Black race" in its Black nationalist meaning. In this he was instead an adherent of Du Bois.

In addition to his academic work Nkrumah found time to study the structure of the various political parties in the U.S. He realized that upon returning to the Gold Coast he would have to put together a political organization capable of waging the struggle for national liberation. He was very much a beginner in this so he researched the party structure of the Republicans, Democrats, Socialists, Communists and Trotskyites. He also studied how political campaigns are run, how the election mechanism functions, and how parties work with various population groups.

Nkrumah not only studied the political process but he got involved in it as well. Specifically, he created the African Students' Association of America and Canada. Admittedly there had been an organization by this name at the University of Pennsylvania previously, but it was more a club for African students, who had not set themselves serious goals. Nkrumah tried to turn this association into an efficacious political organization whose members had rights and duties and worked to implement a program. At his insistence membership in the association was open not only to students but to Africans who were working in the U.S. or Canada as well. It became a forum for heated discussions on the ways in which the colonies could achieve independence. Having become a consistent supporter of pan-African ideas, Nkrumah stood up for his conviction that "unless territorial freedom was ultimately linked up with the Pan-African movement for the liberation of the whole African continent, there would be no hope of freedom and equality for the African and for people of African descent in any part of the world."[2] In 1943 the organisation began to publish a monthly newspaper, *The African Interpreter.* "Through the medium of this newspaper we tried to revive a spirit of nationalism,"[3] Nkrumah later wrote.

Kwame Nkrumah was starting to become a recognizable figure in American public affairs. Various organizations began to invite him to give

[1]*Ghana*, p. 45.
[2]*Ghana*, p. 44.
[3]Ibid.

lectures and speak at public gatherings. The themes he chiefly addressed in such speeches were colonialism and Africa's historical and cultural past. One organization which took an interest in Nkrumah was the Council on African Affairs, established in 1939 at the initiative of Paul Robeson after he made a trip to West Africa and became acquainted with the plight of the indigenous population. Robeson was the soul of this organization. A famous actor whose Othello was unsurpassed on the American stage, he was an educated man who had achieved a Master of Law degree and knew nine languages. The Council on African Affairs brought together people of a variety of political persuasions who were one in their sympathy for the cause of the Black continent's liberation. The organization's headquarters housed an extensive collection of traditional African art and books on Africa. The Council put out a monthly bulletin that informed the public about the state of affairs in the African colonies. Members of the Council raised money to aid the starving population in southern Africa and striking miners in West Africa. The organization's headquarters was the scene of lectures on the continent's problems and receptions for visiting African anti-colonialists.

At the Council's initiative a conference was convened in New York in 1944. Every organization that had shown an interest in Africa's future, including Nkrumah's African Students' Association of America and Canada, took part. The resolution adopted there declared that the U.S. government should act in the spirit of the Atlantic Charter[1] and support any and all forces whose aim was to bring about African independence. A decision was taken to revive the pan-African congresses and to hold the next congress in London immediately following the end of the war.

Kwame Nkrumah knew Paul Robeson well. Robeson contributed a great deal to Nkrumah's understanding of the sources of the racial problem in the United States. Nkrumah's favorite song from the great performer's repertoire was the sad spiritual "Sometimes I Feel Like a Motherless Child". This song spoke to his own feelings. Nkrumah had long felt a strong desire to return to Africa but it was senseless even to give this any thought as long as the war was on. Through Robeson, Kwame Nkrumah got to know many Black artists, writers, composers and

---

[1]A declaration by the heads of the U.S. and British governments signed on August 14, 1941. This declaration outlined, first, the general form and objectives of the war against fascist Germany and her allies, and second, the postwar world order; it declared that no territory would be seized and proclaimed the right of all peoples to choose their form of government. In September 1941 the USSR became a signatory to the Atlantic Charter.

entertainers. He and Richard Wright, the famous Black realist who bravely revealed the ulcers of the "welfare society" in his novels and newspaper articles, were particularly close.

Nkrumah came to believe that as a system capitalism was incapable of guaranteeing genuine equality and freedom. During his studies in the U.S., Nkrumah became acquainted with socialist ideas. This had not come about accidentally, as a type of diversion but was rather the natural result of his search for the answer to a question which deeply concerned him: what was the mechanism governing imperialism's colonial policies? Naturally, no bourgeois studies considered this question scientifically. The answer, as Nkrumah himself noted, was to be found in the works of Marx, Engels and Lenin.

Nkrumah was not the only young African nationalist to be attracted to Marxism-Leninism. Many others were drawn to it by its militant condemnation of imperialism, colonialism and racial and national oppression. Their political lexicons contained such Marxist terms as "alienation," "class struggle," and "exploitation," words that were attractive in their precision and which, it seemed, explained a great deal about the mechanism governing the system of oppression of African peoples. But the majority of Black intellectuals contented themselves with an emotional acknowledgement of the universality of some of the tenets of scientific socialism. Nkrumah went further. In this doctrine he saw an efficacious instrument which could be used by the anti-colonial movement. "During my study in America," he wrote, "the conviction was firmly created in me that a great deal in their [Marx's, Engels' and Lenin's] thought could assist us in the fight against colonialism."[1] Nkrumah was attracted to socialism by its criticism of imperialism, colonialism and racism. The creative and constructive functions of socialism had, as yet, not become the object of his inquiry.

Kwame Nkrumah wrote his first theoretical work on colonial problems in the United States. In this pamphlet, which was later published in 1946 in London under the title *Towards Colonial Freedom,* he attempted to systematize his thoughts on the nature of colonial exploitation from the standpoint of everything he had gleaned during his years of study. "The aim of all colonial governments in Africa and elsewhere has been the struggle for raw materials; and not only this, but the colonies have

---

[1]Kwame Nkrumah, *Consciencism: Philosophy and Ideology for Decolonization and Development with Particular Reference to the African Revolution,* Heinemann, London, 1964, p. 5.

become the dumping ground, and colonial peoples the false recipients, of manufactured goods of the industrialists and capitalists of Great Britain, France, Belgium and other colonial powers... "[1] Nkrumah declared. "Colonialism," he continued, "is, therefore, the policy by which the 'mother country', the colonial power, binds her colonies to herself by political ties with the primary object of promoting her own economic advantages. Such a system depends on the opportunities offered by the natural resources of the colonies and the uses for them suggested by the dominant economic objectives of the colonial power."[2] Nkrumah acknowledged that the most complete and accurate analysis of imperialism and its colonial policies was given in Lenin's *Imperialism, the Highest Stage of Capitalism.* He cited Lenin's definition of imperialism and demonstrated a Marxist understanding of the essence of its policies. "Colonial powers cannot afford to expropriate themselves. And then to imagine that these colonial powers will hand freedom and independence to their colonies on a silver platter without compulsion is the height of folly... "[3] In conclusion, Nkrumah writes: "... Thus the goal of the national liberation mo~ement is the realization of complete and unconditional independence, and the building of a society of peoples in which the free development of each is the condition for the free development of all. Peoples of the colonies, unite! The working men of all countries are behind you."[4] From this, one should probably not overrate the depth of the young African intellectual's knowledge of scientific socialism, but the first steps had been taken.

In May 1945 fascist Germany capitulated. The bloodiest and most terrible war in the history of mankind had not directly touched continental United States. Safe and replete, America stood in sharp contrast to Europe, where so much blood had been spilt and which now lay in ruins. For many Americans the war had seemed like a drawn-out overseas campaign conducted by the "splendid American boys" who were helping to restore democracy in the world. In movie theaters newsreels showed a steady stream of Anglo-Saxon victories over the "Nazi Germans" to the accompaniment of bravura music. The distortion of the war's true nature and the hushing up of the role the Soviet Union played in it gave

[1]Kwame Nkrumah, *Towards Colonial Freedom, Africa in the Struggle Against World Imperialism,* Heinemann, London, 1962, p. xv.

[2]Ibid., p. 2.

[3]Ibid., pp. XVI-XVII.

[4]Ibid., p. 43.

Americans a false understanding of the grandiose events determining the fate of the peoples of the world. The Nazi's first major defeat near Moscow went practically unnoticed, for at that time the newspapers and radio were filled with reports on the Japanese attack on Pearl Harbor, the entry of the U.S. into the war and the activities of the U.S. Navy and Air Force in the Pacific Ocean. But it was impossible to hush up the news of the Red Army's historic victory at Stalingrad in early 1943. The progressive U.S. public (the Communists, first and foremost) distributed correct information about the war, demanded that aid be increased for the Soviet Union, engaged in the main battles against the German fascist hordes, and that the date for the opening of the Second Front be pushed forward. At that time Kwame Nkrumah shared many of the stereotypes foisted on the public by bourgeois propaganda but the very fact that the USSR emerged from the war victorious reinforced his faith in the vitality of socialist ideas.

Immediately following the end of the war and the restoration of normal sea traffic, Kwame Nkrumah packed his bags. In New York harbor he was seen off by the close friends he had made during his long years in America. They all wished him luck in the difficult undertaking he had chosen – fighting for Africa's liberation. Without a shadow of a smile he invited them to visit Africa in ten years' time when colonialism and exploitation would have no place on that continent.

There she was once again, the Statue of Liberty. Much in Nkrumah's understanding of liberty, American-style, had been altered during the past few years. Now he thought it symbolic that the statue stood with her back to America. But then, her gaze was fixed on the boundless ocean, beyond which lay his Africa.

III. Britain

The Liverpool-London train rumbled past city blocks mutilated by bombing and crawled under the gray arch of Euston Station. Kwame Nkrumah stepped onto the platform and looked around. He was supposed to be met but he did not have a great deal of faith that this would actually happen.

Nkrumah hoped to finish his doctoral thesis in philosophy in London and study law. This knowledge might prove useful in his political work in the Gold Coast. He did not know anyone in Britain, so once again he was faced with the urgent problem of finding work and housing. Before leaving the United States, Nkrumah had read several articles exposing colonialism and imperialism by George Padmore, a West Indian journalist who resided in London. Padmore's ideas were in many ways consonant with his own. He sent Padmore a letter in which he gave a brief account of himself, informed Padmore of the date he was arriving in London and asked him to meet the train if that was convenient.

Padmore came to the station. He took Nkrumah to a dormitory run by the West African Students Union, an organization set up to provide assistance to African students abroad, and asked him to keep in touch. Thus began a new period in Nkrumah's life.

He spent his first days in London looking for a flat. Many times the landladies he went to see slammed the door in his face as soon as they caught a glimpse of their "colored" visitor who, on top of everything else, did not give the impression of being solvent. In the end he found a small room at 60 Burleigh Road. Here Nkrumah was to spend the next two and a half years.

Work on his doctoral thesis had to continue. For classes in philosophy Kwame Nkrumah enrolled in University College. He was fascinated by logical positivism, a variety of neo-positivism, that was fashionable at that time in the West. Nkrumah disagreed with the extremes of "worldly" materialism and mysticized idealism. Logical positivism interested him because it attempted to "reconcile" materialism and idealism. His study of logical positivism left its mark on his thinking. In many works he made extensive use of the symbolic and mathematical logic characteristic of that philosophical school. He always adhered to the "principle of pragmatism" which defines the meaning of truth by its practical utility and defines ideas as instruments of action. Nkrumah believed that ideas arising in the minds of "great men" transformed reality.

In his discussion of Nkrumah's philosophical studies, the British historian Basil Davidson cites the opinion of Sir Alfred Ayer, one of the world's leading neo-positivists: " '. . . I can't honestly say . . . that I thought Nkrumah a first-class philosopher. I liked him and enjoyed talking to him but he did not seem to me to have an analytical mind. He wanted the answers too quickly. I think part of the trouble may have been that he wasn't concentrating very hard on his thesis. It was a way of marking time until the opportunity came for him to return to Ghana.' "[1] Perhaps the professor was right. The events then taking place around the world did not leave much time for the study of "pure" philosophy; they demanded political action.

Kwame Nkrumah arrived in London in 1945, one month after the end of the Second World War. In San Francisco the UN Charter, which determined the main trends in postwar international relations, had been signed by representatives of the states participating in the constitutent conference there. There was a powerful revolutionary surge throughout the world, brought on by the defeat of the most reactionary and openly chauvinistic forces of world imperialism – the fascist bloc countries. The prerequisites for socialist revolution sprang up in a number of European and Asian countries, which signified a radical shift in the balance of power towards socialism. Progressive forces demanding that radical social changes be made in their countries gathered strength in capitalist Europe.

This shift to the left affected Britain, too. In 1945 the first parliamentary elections were held since the war. The Conservatives, led by Winston Churchill, suffered a crushing defeat. The Labour government of Clement Attlee came to power, having made extensive use of the socialist phraseology so popular with the masses and promised substantial changes in both home and foreign (including colonial) policies. "Let Us Face the Future"

[1]Basil Davidson, *Black Star . . .*, p. 47.

was the title of the Labour program. Nkrumah took this to mean that the time had come when decisive action would be taken.

A few months after his arrival in England Kwame Nkrumah became the vice-president of the West African Students' Union. He transformed what had chiefly been a philanthropic organization into a political association for African students. It petitioned the Colonial Office to improve living conditions for the indigenous population of Africa.

At that time Nkrumah's work to bring about Africa's liberation was closely linked to pan-Africanism. He was highly involved in the preparations for and running of the first postwar Pan-African congress. Pan-Africanism had a great influence on the development of the struggle against colonialism on the African continent. Nkrumah came to the conclusion that a political association of independent West African states must be formed.

Nkrumah gained a greater understanding of socialist ideas through his association with the pan-African movement, whose radical elements called on Africa to take the path of socialism during the years of the global postwar democratic surge. The ideas of "democratic socialism" were a powerful force in pan-Africanism at that time. They were advocated by George Padmore, who aspired to be the mentor of young radical African intellectuals. He denied the necessity of unity with the Soviet Union and other anti-imperialist forces in the fight against colonialism, a view which had brought about Padmore's break with the Communist International in 1935. Nevertheless, he made use of several Marxist-Leninist tenets in his critique of imperialism and colonialism. The influence Padmore's ideas had on Nkrumah was strong and initially the young philosopher absorbed socialist ideas as they were interpreted by reformists. To no small degree this was facilitated by his association with several prominent members of the ruling Labour Party. Nevertheless, the fact remains that Nkrumah had familiarized himself with socialist theory and comprehended its creative essence. It was clear to him that Africa's future independent development should be linked to socialism.

George Padmore and W. E. B. Du Bois were primarily responsible for convening the Fifth Pan-African Congress which was scheduled to be held in Manchester in October 1945. As Secretary of the Organization Committee, Kwame Nkrumah threw himself into preparations for the Congress. Together with South African writer Peter Abrahams he wrote hundreds of letters to various political organizations, trade unions and cooperatives in Africa and the West Indies explaining the goals of the upcoming meeting and the tasks facing the anti-colonial movement. In addition to the letters, he and Abrahams prepared materials and final documents for the Congress. His adherence to the ideals of pan-Africanism, his burning desire to take part in politics, his erudition and the fact that he was personally acquainted with prominent figures in the pan-African movement all guaranteed that Nkrumah would play one of the most important roles at the Manchester congress.

The Fifth Pan-African Congress was opened on October 15, 1945 under the chairmanship of the 77-year-old W. E. B. Du Bois, the "Grand Old Man" as he was called by those attending the Congress. The date had not been chosen at random. A World Federation of Trade Unions conference had been held in Paris in September and October: thus, many trade unionists from Africa were able to go to Manchester. All in all there were over two hundred delegates and observers. The congress became an important landmark in the history of pan-Africanism. Whereas previously pan-African congresses had for the most part been convened and run by Black intellectuals whose main concern was racial discrimination, most of those attending the Fifth Pan-African Congress were African trade unionists, politicians, workers and students. In Kwame Nkrumah's words, "They represented re-awakening African political consciousness."[1]

Nkrumah was the keynote speaker at the third and fourth sessions of the congress where the economic and social problems of the West African colonies and questions concerning the organization of nationalist movements in that region were discussed. The resolution, presented by Nkrumah and unanimously approved by the delegates, read: "In connection with the political situation, the Congress observed: a) That since the advent of British, French, Belgian and other European nations in West Africa, there has been regression instead of progress as a result of systematic exploitation by these alien imperialist powers. The claims of 'partnership,' 'trusteeship,' 'guardianship,' and the 'mandate system,' do not serve the political wishes of the people of West Africa . . . ; c) That the introduction of pretentious constitutional reforms in the West African territories are nothing but spurious attempts on the part of alien imperialist powers to continue the political enslavement of the peoples."[2]

It was a congress of the young generation of fighters for the liberation

---

[1]Kwame Nkrumah, *Revolutionary Path,* International Publishers, New York, 1973, p. 42.

[2]Quoted in: George Padmore, *Pan-Africanism or Communism? The Coming Struggle for Africa,* Dennis Dobson, London, 1956, pp. 163-164.

of Africa. Due to the surge in the democratic movement throughout the world and the achievements of socialism, on the one hand, and the composition of the delegations attending the congress on the other, the ideas of pan-Africanism began to be perceived as the ideas that would unify all the peoples of the African continent in the fight against imperialism and colonialism.

As the congress drew to a close the delegates adopted several important declarations. The most radical of these – *A Declaration to the Colonial Peoples* – was the work of Kwame Nkrumah. Rejecting the reformist orientation of the first pan-African congresses, the declaration called on all Africans to unite in the struggle for national liberation. This document also reflects Nkrumah's growing political maturity. It read, in part:

We affirm the right of all colonial peoples to control their own destiny. All colonies must be free from foreign imperialist control, whether political or economic.

The peoples of the colonies must have the right to elect their own Governments, without restrictions from foreign Powers. We say to the peoples of the colonies that they must fight for these ends by all means at their disposal.

The object of imperialist Powers is to exploit. By granting the right to colonial peoples to govern themselves that object is defeated. Therefore, the struggle for political power by colonial and subject peoples is the first step towards, and the necessary prerequisite to, complete social, economic and political emancipation. The Fifth Pan-African Congress therefore calls on the workers and farmers of the Colonies to organize effectively. Colonial workers must be in the front of the battle against imperialism. Your weapons – the strike and the boycott – are invincible.

We also call upon the intellectuals and professional classes of the colonies to awaken to their responsibilities. By fighting for trade union rights, the right to form cooperatives, freedom of the press, assembly, demonstration and strike, freedom to print and read the literature which is necessary for the education of the masses, you will be using the only means by which your liberation will be won and maintained. Today there is only one road to effective action – the organization of the masses. And in that organization the educated colonials must join. Colonial and subject peoples of the world, Unite.[1]

[1]*Ideologies of Liberation in Black Africa*, 1856-1970 ..., pp. 760-761.

The final phrase was not just a felicitous ending. It reflected Nkrumah's conviction that the various detachments of the anti-colonial movement had to be united if imperialism was to be combatted. His position was positively received by the majority of delegates. The Fifth Pan-African Congress sent messages of solidarity to the peoples of India, Indonesia and Vietnam who were then fighting for national independence.

The participants in the congress favored a socialist future for independent Africa; however, they rejected violence as a means of achieving this goal. The Fifth Pan-African Congress was an event of great importance in Nkrumah's life. The congress's ideals – anti-colonialism, anti-imperialism and non-violence – were to constitute the basis of his political philosophy.

In order to implement the decisions of the congress a group of West Africans set up a regional organization, the West African National Secretariat, headquartered in London. Kwame Nkrumah was elected General Secretary. The secretariat's primary responsibility was to develop and implement plans for a West African federation of independent states. Nkrumah linked the creation of such a federation to the liberation of Africa as a whole. As the most highly developed region in the continent both economically and politically, West Africa, in Nkrumah's opinion, was destined to be a bridgehead for liberation from colonialism. The secretariat's program stated, "The day when West Africa, as one united country, pulls itself from imperialist oppression and exploitation it will pull the rest of Africa with her."[1]

A small room at 94 Gray's Inn Road became the young nationalists' headquarters. Here preparations were made for a meeting between leaders of the British and French West African colonies at which they planned to discuss urgent problems and develop a concrete program of joint action. The need for such a meeting was dictated in part by the fact that the French-speaking Africans had not been represented at the Manchester congress. Kwame Nkrumah made a trip to Paris where he met with Leopold Senghor, Félix Houphouet-Boigny, Lamine Gueye and Sourous Apithy, African deputies to the French National Assembly.

The conference took place in London in late August and early September 1946. Senghor and Apithy came as representatives of the French West African colonies. The delegates to the conference approved the decisions of the Fifth Pan-African Congress and joined it in declaring that a struggle should be waged not just for self-government within the framework of

[1]Imanuel Geiss, *The Pan-African Movement*, p. 413.

the colonial territories but for the formation of a West African federation as well. The resolution that was adopted demanded immediate and absolute self-government for the peoples of West Africa.

Nkrumah went to Paris a second time and once again those with whom he spoke assured him that pan-African ideals had their full support. It would seem that every obstacle had been overcome and in the independent Africa of the future there would be no place for borders artificially created by imperialist powers. Lagos, Nigeria was chosen as the site for a new and more representative conference of those who advocated the creation of a united, independent Africa. There, in 1948, the West African National Conference would be held.

One of the secretariat's tasks was to draw the attention of the European public to the plight of the indigenous population in the British African colonies. Kwame Nkrumah considered this a matter of great importance. Those who passed through Trafalgar Square or strolled in Hyde Park in those days frequently saw a passionately gesticulating African speaking before a crowd. Prominent Labourites sometimes came to these gatherings. They spoke with heartfelt conviction of social justice and reforms while calling for patience, wisdom and calm. But the gap between the words and the deeds of the Labour government was becoming increasingly apparent to Africans. "Our hopes in the Labour Party were completely dashed to pieces," Nkrumah recalled, "in fact we saw little difference between Labour colonial policy and that of the Tories."[1]

Kwame Nkrumah, a great believer in the power of the printed word, convinced the members of the secretariat that an official organ was needed. They managed to scrape together fifty pounds and in March 1946 the first issue of *The New African,* a monthly newspaper, came off the presses. The newspaper's subhead, "The Voice of the Awakened Africa," and its motto, "For Unity and Absolute Independence," left no one in any doubt as to its orientation. The topical and pointed articles it printed met with a warm response from educated Africans residing in Britain. Soon, however, *The New African* folded due to a lack of funds.

Together with other like-minded persons, Nkrumah set up the Coloured Workers Association of Great Britain. However, many Africans who had settled in Britain for one reason or another belonged to the category of the unemployed rather than that of workers. Nkrumah became a frequent visitor to two dismal districts in London's East End, Stepney and White-

---

[1] *Ghana,* p. 58.

chapel. Here, in tumbledown buildings which looked more like abandoned warehouses than blocks of flats the Black pariahs of this "free" society lived in horribly crowded conditions. Nkrumah travelled to other British industrial centers as well and investigated the conditions under which these outcasts without rights lived. In the eyes of the people he spoke with he saw despair and, more frequently, utter indifference. The ideas for which African intellectuals in London ate, slept and breathed had little relevance in their lives. They needed help in finding work or returning home. This was where the West African National Secretariat directed its efforts although, at the same time, it did not neglect to draw the most politically conscious workers into political work.

Financially, Nkrumah and his friends were not much better off than the "coloured workers" whom they so tried to help. Even heated discussion in the offices of the secretariat could not always warm the freezing, half-starved functionaries. Temporarily putting aside their plans for reshaping the continent, they would take to the streets of London in hopes of finding a few pieces of coal which had fallen from a lorry. They had nothing with which to buy fuel. Nkrumah dined in the cheapest restaurants. Coming home after midnight he would eat whatever food his landlady had left out for him. In return, he washed all the dirty dishes for the house.

Kwame Nkrumah decided to create an organization made up of likeminded activists capable of directing the secretariat's activities as its ruling core. The organization which combined the traits of a political party, a conspiratorial sect and a Masonic lodge was called the Circle. Its motto was the three S's – Service, Sacrifice, Suffering. The members of the organization were obliged to maintain themselves and the Circle "as the Revolutionary Vanguard of the Struggle for West African Unity and National Independence" and "support the idea and claims of the All West African National Congress in its struggle to create and maintain a Union of African Socialist Republics ... " The members of the organization swore to irrevocably obey and act upon the instructions of the "Grand Council" and accept the leadership of Kwame Nkrumah. Furthermore they promised never to betray the Circle's secrets or plans and not to use the organization to further their private interests. In order to prove their devotion to the organization, its members were supposed to fast from sunrise to sunset on the 21st day of each month.[1] Despite its somewhat mystical trappings the Circle fulfilled quite practi-

---

[1] *Revolutionary Path,* pp. 47–48.

cal functions in terms of organizing meetings, conferences, lectures and discussions. The idea of setting up the Union of African Socialist Republics was apparently borrowed from Awooner Renner, a talented writer from the Gold Coast who published a book entitled *The West African Soviet Union* in London in 1946. At the end of the 1920s Awooner Renner had lived in the Soviet Union where he had been a member of the Writers' Union and participated in the International Conference of Proletarian and Revolutionary Writers in Moscow. In his book he proposed that all the colonies in West Africa be united in a federation of socialist states which would take the impressive example of the USSR as its model. It was the author's opinion that the fight for unity and independence should be led by the West African National Congress, or rather, by that organization, reestablished: a political organization by that name had been founded in the Gold Coast by Casely-Hayford in 1920 but to all intents and purposes it had ceased to exist after his death in 1930. When the representatives of the British and French colonies met in London they decided to revive the West African National Congress.

More than two years had passed since Kwame Nkrumah had come to Britain. Anti-colonial organizations had been created and were functioning smoothly although, admittedly, they were as yet limited to the territory of the colonial power. Ties had been established with nationalists from the French colonies and together they had outlined their common goals. Now Nkrumah concentrated his efforts on realizing his dreams of organizing a conference to be held on African soil and attended by delegations from all the political movements which supported the liberation of the continent. This conference was slated to be held in Lagos in 1948. If it lived up to expectations it would become the launching pad for a broad anti-colonial movement in West Africa. If it was primarily Nkrumah's personality that had been shaped while he was in the United States, in Britain his growth as a political figure occurred. He became one of the leaders of the pan-African movement.

At the height of the work to organize the conference, Kwame Nkrumah received a letter from the Gold Coast. Nkrumah's old friend, Ako Adjei, was writing to inform him that a political organization called the United Gold Coast Convention (UGCC) which demanded that Africans be granted the right to govern the country, had been formed there. As he knew of Nkrumah's organizational abilities, Adjei had proposed that he be offered the post of General Secretary and the Executive Committee had given its consent. Should he accept the offer Nkrumah could count on a monthly salary of 100 pounds.

The offer was tempting. He was being given a chance to try to put his ideals into practice. But he was troubled by the fact that he was being offered such high remuneration for his services. To Nkrumah, who was accustomed to a more than modest lifestyle, comfortable circumstances and revolutionary activity seemed incompatible. He decided to make some inquiries into the country's political situation and the United Gold Coast Convention. Nkrumah gathered from what he was told by a teacher he knew at Oxford who had recently visited the colony that the activities of this reformist organization – which had been set up by a bourgeois "elite" – had little in common with those of a real anti-colonial movement. Moreover, it was confined to the excessively narrow framework of the Gold Coast, in his opinion, and did not seek to coordinate its actions with those of other organizations on the level of Africa as a whole. Meanwhile, he received yet another letter from one of the founders of the Convention, Joseph B. Danquah, who earnestly entreated him to accept the post. Kwame Nkrumah believed that he did not have the right to decide this question alone, so he put it before the West African National Secretariat. Having weighed all the pros and cons the members of the secretariat recommended that he accept the offer. In turn, Nkrumah promised never to compromise with reactionary and reformist tendencies within the UGCC leadership. Having received the money for his passage from the Executive Committee of the Convention and said goodbye to his friends, Kwame Nkrumah set out for Liverpool on November 14, 1947 in order to take the next ship home. He had spent a long time searching for the golden fleece. Now he was certain that it had to be sought in Africa.

In Liverpool he found that his political activities in England had not gone unnoticed by the British police. During the lengthy interrogations to which he was subjected, he was amazed at how well informed the police officials were as to his political views, activities and acquaintances. The police were particularly interested in the meetings he had had with British Communists. Churchill had already delivered his speech at Fulton, Missouri, and the wheels of the cold war machine had begun to turn. In the end, however, Nkrumah received permission to leave.

IV. "Self-Government Now!"

The steamship on which Kwame Nkrumah travelled made its first call in Freetown – the center of the British colony of Sierra Leone. Nkrumah decided to remain there for two weeks in order to establish personal ties with the country's nationalists and pave the way for the pan-African conference in Lagos. He spoke at a few rallies and student assemblies on the unity of the West African colonies in the struggle for independence. From there Nkrumah went on to Liberia. This visit was a flop: President Tubman was away and high-ranking government officials gave Nkrumah to understand that Liberia would not be an active participant in his pan-African undertakings. With that his diplomatic mission came to an end, as did his money. On the last leg of his journey to the Gold Coast, Nkrumah's berth was the dirty cargo deck of a steamship. In Takoradi he learned that his reputation had long preceded him. A Black immigration official took Nkrumah off to one side, away from his European colleagues, and excitedly informed him that many Africans had heard of him and were impatiently awaiting his arrival.

Kwame Nkrumah did not hasten to meet the leaders of the United Gold Coast Convention. He decided to first acquaint himself with the situation in the country from which he had absented himself for so many years, gather his thoughts and, finally, just relax a little. So he spent the first two weeks in Tarkwa at the home of a close friend. While he was there his mother came from Nkroful to see him. Each was surprised by the changes that had been wrought in the other. Nyanibah's hair had turned gray and her eyesight was now poor. Nkrumah, too, had changed. So much, in fact, that his mother barely recognized him. Mother and son spent long hours telling each other about their lives.

Nkrumah's main source of information was from the local newspapers that his host brought him. Of the foreign news, Nkrumah's attention was drawn to a report from India (already liberated from colonialism)

34

on the death of Mohandas Karamchand Gandhi, who had been assassinated by a fanatic from a chauvinistic Hindu organisation. Gandhi's theory of nonviolence as a form of mass resistance to colonial oppression had long interested Nkrumah and he held most of its tenets. But he was primarily interested in local news. The country's attention had been focussed on the splendid funeral of the chief of the Gas, Nii Tackie Tawai II. Part of the ceremony involved the sacrificing of animals whose blood was splashed over the grave. Thousands of Gas were inconsolable at the loss of their ruler. It would seem that old, traditional Africa had not been affected by the twentieth century. But no, there had been some changes, too. One Nii Kwabena Bonne, who was performing the duties of chief, had organized a campaign of protest against the exorbitant prices on imported goods. Shops owned by European companies had been boycotted. Over 600 demonstrators had marched through the streets of Accra carrying signs that read "We Will Not Buy!" and "Wait Until Prices Are Reduced!". In the end the foreigners had been forced to back down. *The African Morning Post* wrote, "The Gold Coast African is today awake; . . . and there is reason to believe he will sleep no more."[1]

Yes, much had changed in the Gold Coast in the years Nkrumah had spent in the U.S. and Britain. It was no longer the country which the colonial administration's annual reports had called a "model" and "peace-loving" colony making "orderly and constitutional progress" towards self-government.[2]

The victory of the anti-Hitler coalition, the expansion of socialism beyond the framework of one country, the formation of the world socialist system, and the increasing influence of progressive forces in capitalist countries weakened world imperialism and created circumstances favorable to the successful expansion of the African people's national liberation struggle. Big changes had occurred in Africa itself. The Second World War had affected the Black continent which had until then stood on the sidelines of world events. Experiencing a shortage of resources and strategic raw materials, Britain was forced to lay the foundations for industry in its colonies. The Gold Coast was Britain's main source of manganese ore and bauxite. The mining of industrial diamonds, gold, and valuable types of timber had seen a significant increase during the war

[1]Quoted in: Kwame Nkrumah, *I Speak of Freedom*, Heinemann, London, 1961, p. 4.
[2]Dennis Austin, *Politics in Ghana: 1946–1960*, Oxford University Press, London, 1964, p. 3.

years. The war had severed normal economic ties: the import of industrial and agricultural goods from Britain had been sharply curtailed. This led to the development of a few branches of the food and manufacturing industries in the Gold Coast. This, in turn, brought about important social changes. The numerical strength of two new social forces – the working class and the national bourgeoisie – increased. The decay of clan-tribal relations led to the growth of cities. During the war the population of Accra nearly doubled. The same process occurred in Kumasi, Sekondi-Takoradi and other cities. Sixty-five thousand inhabitants of the Gold Coast fought in Somalia, Ethiopia and Burma as members of the British armed forces. Their participation in the international fight against fascism broadened their political outlook and opened their eyes to the injustice and unlawfulness of the oppression of one people by another. All of these factors helped raise the population's level of social and political activity and create a national consciousness.

At the end of the 1940s the objective prerequisites for the creation of a broad anti-colonial front had been met. Various population groups occupying different positions in society keenly felt the sting of colonial oppression.

Though small in number the working class was the best organized class with its trade unions, united in the Trade Union Congress. The level of occupational skill within the working class was not high. That class primarily consisted of unskilled workers, yesterday's peasants, now employed in the mining industry. Their standard of living was extremely low. The postwar inflation and the constant rise in food prices had the most telling effect on the working class. At the same time the new conditions helped bring about the workers' gradual liberation from the narrow-mindedness of the tribe and their political consciousness began to develop.

The peasants suffered from the inordinately high taxes levied by the colonial administration. In 1943 the British authorities introduced direct taxation which Sir Alan Burns, then Governor of the colony, called "one of the inevitable results of civilisation."[1] Rural areas were without schools and hospitals. As the peasants increasingly came in contact with the city they began to realize that they lacked even the most basic things.

For the Gold Coast's small bourgeoisie the way was barred to industry. They primarily made their living from small-scale commerce and cacao

---

[1]*Great Britain and Ghana, Documents of Ghana History, 1807–1957,* ed. by Y. E. Metcalfe, Thomas Nelson & Sons, Ltd., London, 1964, p. 667.

bean production. But here, too, the national bourgeoisie did not feel that they were masters of the situation as they were continually under pressure from British monopolies.

Politically, the most active force in the Gold Coast was the national intelligentsia. It grew fairly quickly, first, because the needs of the colonial economy were increasing and second, as a result of the colony's constant struggle to expand the educational system. Admittedly, the majority of the country's intellectuals were cut off from the people. But their attachment to Western culture did not signify their reconciliation to the growth of colonial exploitation.

The youth of the Gold Coast were opposed to colonialism. This was particularly true of those who did not wish to remain in the village, which was backward, dominated by traditions that had outlived their time, and ruled by chiefs and elders who refused to recognize anything new; these young people departed for the city in hopes of finding work. Due to the influx of young people the urban population grew quickly in the 1940s. There were not enough jobs to go around, however, and the majority of these youths suffered from social dislocation.

An analysis of social, economic and political conditions in the Gold Coast reveals that at the end of the 1940s the bulk of the population believed that independence alone could alter their situation. The British, on the other hand, did not even let the thought that their mastery might soon come to an end enter their heads. The Governor of the colony declared that "ninety-nine per cent of the inhabitants of the Gold Coast are perfectly satisfied with the Government in its present form" and that the Africans "realise the immense debt of gratitude they owe to Europeans for the work they have done, and are doing, in the Gold Coast ... "[1]

At the same time the British tried not to lose the initiative. In an attempt to damp down the growing anti-colonialism, Britain resorted to making minor political concessions to the Africans. The Labour government demagogically proclaimed that it was embarking on a "new" course vis-a-vis the colonies. In the Gold Coast a "constitution" named the Burns Constitution in honor of the Governor went into force in April 1946. Naturally, no Africans had been invited to participate in its drafting and it primarily concerned election procedures for the so-called Legislative Council – a consultative body which advised the governor. Although Africans formally had a majority in this 31 member council they did not

---

[1] *Great Britain and Ghana,* p. 665.

possess any real power. High property qualifications had been established for those members of the Legislative Council appointed by the Governor or elected by the tribal chiefs. Knowledge of English was also essential. These conditions for membership were designed to give the conservative, pro-Western elite an edge. The spearhead for the interests of this group was the United Gold Coast Convention which had offered Kwame Nkrumah the post of General Secretary in the hopes that it could make use of his more than ten years' experience in politics abroad and his prestige within the pan-African movement.

The United Gold Coast Convention, established in August 1947 at the initiative of one of the biggest entrepreneurs in the country, an exporter of timber and cacao, George Grant, brought together conservative members of the urban and rural elite. The leaders of the UGCC – rich merchants and lawyers – thought that the masses were not ready for independence, and did nothing to further their political education. The organization wanted to ensure that "by all legitimate and constitutional means the control and direction of Government [should] within the shortest time possible pass into the hands of the people and their Chiefs."[1] In practice this meant trying to get new concessions from the British for the benefit of the country's privileged groups. The colonial authorities were not alarmed by the establishment of this organization because its social essence was obvious. Once he took up his post as head of the UGCC, Kwame Nkrumah began to seek support from the masses rather than from the British. He was resolved to radicalize the organization even if he had to go against the wishes of its conservative leadership to do so. In January 1948 he devised a plan for reorganizing the UGCC, a plan which, in essence, envisaged its transformation into a mass-based political party. Nkrumah believed that the self-government movement should involve not only the large coastal towns but the remote regions of the Northern Territories, Ashanti and Trans-Volta Togoland. The trade unions, women's and other public organizations should unite under the aegis of the UGCC and act within the framework of its program. Sunday political education classes for the masses had to be set up throughout the country. Demonstrations, boycotts and strikes should become the main instruments of struggle for independence. The Convention's leadership did not, in principle, object to the General Secretary's plans, believing, apparently, that their immensity doomed them to failure. It was proposed that he set up his headquarters in the small, remote town of Saltpond.

[1]*Ghana*, p. 69.

Nkrumah made long trips around the country in an ancient car which the organization had given him to use and spoke at innumerable gatherings. Within a few months he had set up hundreds of branches of the UGCC. Nkrumah made his way to the far corners of the Gold Coast by hitchhiking and frequently by walking (the car was forever breaking down); the forest provided him with lodging for the night. Using simple language which every peasant, fisherman and worker could understand, he explained the movement's goals and tasks. His manner contrasted sharply with that of the pretentious Black gentlemen from Accra who always maintained a certain distance when they had occasion to meet with those who now made up Nkrumah's audience. These unaffected people shared their simple food with him and became ardent supporters and members of the UGCC.

Nkrumah realized what an explosive force African youth represented – on the whole unemployed and unhappy with their social status. Thousands of young men who had received a primary school education and did not wish to remain in the village with its archaic social structure where behavior was strictly regulated by obsolete traditions, moved to the city. The overwhelming majority had neither a trade nor a job. The blessings of city life were unattainable for these lads. The call for self-government gave them hope. Assisted by his friends Krobo Edusei, Kofi Baako and Kojo Botsio, Nkrumah set up youth organizations all over the country. They were later consolidated under the Committee on Youth Organization, formally part of the UGCC but in reality an independent political organization under the direction of Kwame Nkrumah.

On February 28, 1948, African members of the armed forces who had fought in the Second World War and were now demobilized organized a peaceful march to Christianborg Castle, the British Governor's residence. There they planned to deliver a petition demanding the benefits which had been promised them during the war and assistance in finding work. As the demonstrators approached the castle the police opened fire. The order that brought about the bloody carnage was issued by a British officer.

The news of the crime quickly spread throughout Accra. Africans began to vent their anger on the hated European merchants. Their stores were wrecked, their cars were smashed. The warehouses of the largest European monopoly in Africa, the United Africa Company, were set on fire. A state of emergency was declared in the country and the British called out the troops to restore order in Accra. As a result of the clashes 20 people died and 237 were injured. In a radio broadcast the Governor announced that a "Communist plot" was afoot in the country. The British estimated that property worth two million pounds sterling had been destroyed in the rioting, but for them the damage was far greater. The last remnants of faith in the lawfulness and necessity of colonial rule had been destroyed.

The UGCC had not had anything to do with these events. Nkrumah, for one, had been in Saltpond at the time. Nevertheless, he and five other members of the Convention's leadership were arrested by order of the Governor and exiled under guard to the remote Northern Territories. Nkrumah spent approximately six weeks in solitary confinement in a small hut under the watchful eyes of policemen. Loneliness, however, did not weigh upon him too greatly. Now he had time calmly to analyze the political situation in the country and to make corrections in his plans for further action. Moreover, he was delivered from his fellow prisoners' laments and reproaches which he had constantly been forced to hear when they shared a cell in Kumasi. The others blamed Nkrumah for everything. Eventually, all six were taken to Accra where they appeared before the commission investigating the reasons for the recent disturbances in the "model" colony. Named after its chairman, it was known as the Watson Commission.

Of the six, the commission was most interested in Nkrumah. It had an extensive dosier containing materials on his activities in the U.S. and Britain along with some "damning" pieces of evidence which had been confiscated at the time of his arrest – a blank membership card for the Communist Party of Great Britain and the Circle's charter. After questioning him at length the commission came to the conclusion that "Mr. Kwame Nkrumah has never abandoned his aims for a Union of West African Soviet Socialist Republics and has not abandoned his foreign affiliations connected with these aims."[1] Clearly, the facts had been juggled in order to meet a provocative aim – to uncover a "Communist threat" in Africa. Neither in the documents he authored nor in the speeches he gave did Nkrumah ever use the phrase "Soviet republics." Seditious ideas were also uncovered in the UGCC reorganization plan devised by Nkrumah and approved by the Working Committee. In its report the commission noted that "Mr. Nkrumah boldly proposes a program which is all too familiar to those who have studied the technique of countries that have fallen the victims of communist enslavement."[2]

[1]*Ghana*, p. 87.
[2]Ibid.

At the same time, in order to weaken the growing anti-imperialist movement and bring about a split in its ranks, the Watson Commission declared itself to be of the opinion that the Burns Constitution, which had catered to the tribal chiefs, was not appropriate to the new conditions prevailing in the country. It recommended that a committee made up of Africans be formed to draw up a new, "more democratic" constitution which would provide for broad participation by the privileged sections of the population in governing the colony. Such a committee, made up of chiefs and members of the UGCC leadership, was formed: all forty of its members were appointed by the Governor. The committee was headed by Henley Coussey, a fifty-five year old successful lawyer.

The UGCC leadership, worried by Nkrumah's radicalism and growing popularity, particularly among young people, hastened to dissociate itself from the General Secretary and his far-reaching plans. The Working Committee dismissed Nkrumah from his post. He was offered one hundred pounds to cover his expenses if he would return to England. Nkrumah declined. Next he was offered the post of party treasurer. It was not hard to size up the situation. If Nkrumah refused the post he would be excluded from the leadership. If he accepted it his activities would be limited to the area of UGCC finances. Kwame Nkrumah chose the second option but by no means on the conditions set by the gentlemen from the leadership. A break was not yet unavoidable. There was still work to be done in setting up the Committee on Youth Organization and launching, in spite of the resistance shown by the Convention's leadership, a newspaper that would, in Nkrumah's words, become "the vanguard of the movement and its chief propagandist, agitator, mobilizer and political educationist."[1]

The first issue of *The Accra Evening News,* printed on one sheet of paper, came out in early September 1948. Money was always a problem. The paper had to be composed and printed manually. This was frequently done by Nkrumah himself and four or five helpers. All the same the new publication was enormously popular. Crowds gathered outside the editorial offices to obtain copies of the latest issue. Readings for the illiterate were arranged on the streets. The paper's mottos – "We have the right to live as men," "We have the right to govern ourselves" and "We prefer self-government with danger to servitude in tranquility" – were understandable to all and acted as a call to action. The headline of one article, "Self-Government Now," became the most popular slogan in the country.

It was written on houses and fences. The headlines Nkrumah wrote were of great significance in the mobilization of the masses. They explained the strategic and tactical tasks of the anti-colonial movement in everyday, easily understood language.

The rift between Nkrumah and the conservative leadership of the UGCC deepened. Now the Committee on Youth Organization became the latter's main target. Under Nkrumah's leadership it had become more and more politically active and, refusing to bow to the recommendations of the Working Committee, had increasingly taken on the characteristics of an independent organization. Finally, at a committee conference held in June 1949 in Tarkwa, the decision was taken to break with the UGCC and form an independent political party. At Nkrumah's suggestion it was named the Convention People's Party (CPP). The party's program was hammered out at the same forum. It set as the party's goals "to fight relentlessly by all constitutional means for the achievement of full 'Self-Government Now' for the chiefs and people of the Gold Coast" and "to serve as the vigorous conscious political vanguard for removing all forms of oppression and for the establishment of a democratic government."[1]

On June 12, 1949 a mass rally was held under a sunny sky at the Arena stadium in Accra. There Kwame Nkrumah told sixty thousand of his supporters of his differences with the UGCC on the question of self-government. Then he announced the birth of the Convention People's Party which, he declared, would wage a determined fight to the victorious end.

The ranks of the new party quickly grew. The local UGCC organizations which Nkrumah had set up either went over to the CPP or collapsed. The personal popularity of the party's Chairman, too, grew quickly. This was in no small part due to his great oratorical skills and his ability to establish and maintain a rapport with his audience. "As an orator, Nkrumah brings all his theatrical skill into play," wrote Bankole Timothy, who knew him well, "he is a born actor, who plays on the emotions of his audience. For effect, he uses his hands while speaking ... "[2] But Nkrumah did not just speak vividly and emotionally. He talked about the people's most pressing problems and he did so in words that everybody could understand. Moreover, rather than shunning customs and superstitions

---

[1]*Ghana,* p. 101.

[2]Bankole Timothy, *Kwame Nkrumah: His Rise to Power,* George Allen & Unwin, Ltd., London, 1963, p. 124.

he used them to attract new supporters. The rallies at which Nkrumah spoke frequently began with the sacrifice of a sheep or goat to the gods and ancestors. They ended with a rush to join the ranks of the CPP. The party's red, white and green standard flew in the remotest parts of the country. Young men and women paraded about in shirts and dresses emblazoned with the party's colors and featuring Nkrumah's portrait, which enterprising merchants had quickly produced for sale.

Nkrumah strove to impart a mass character to the CPP. He stressed that the party should reflect the interests of the people as a whole. As he explained in his autobiography, "... we had excluded no one. For if a national movement is to succeed, every man and woman of goodwill must be allowed to play a part."[1] By 1950 the CPP had a membership of over one million. As the party drew on many different social groups, it could express the interests of all the people of the Gold Coast, a place where class differences were pronounced only on the question of independence. "Seek ye first the political kingdom and all things shall be added unto you,"[2] Nkrumah would tell his supporters, paraphrasing the Gospel. At this stage of the anti-imperialist revolution the interests of the workers, petty bourgeoisie, peasants and intelligentsia concurred. They all wanted to attain the "political kingdom" but the hopes they had attached to that kingdom differed.

The method of waging struggle for political independence Nkrumah chose was *positive action*. At the basis of this method were the principles of non-violent resistance developed by Mahatma Gandhi and first applied by him in the *satyagraha* or campaign of civil disobedience carried out at the beginning of the century in South Africa where Gandhi led the Indians' struggle against racial discrimination and oppression. For him non-violence combined active protest and tolerance toward the adversary. Nkrumah had long been engaged in elaborating these ideas. Due in part to his influence, the Fifth Pan-African Congress recommended that positive action without violence be the main method used in combating colonialism. Nkrumah himself gave the following definition of positive action: "Positive Action ... the adoption of all legitimate and constitutional means by which we could attack the forces of imperialism in the country. The weapons were legitimate political agitation, newspaper and educational campaigns and, as a last resort, the constitutional application

---

[1]*Ghana*, p. 109.
[2]*Ghana*, p. 164.

of strikes, boycotts and non-cooperation based on the principle of absolute non-violence ... "[1]

In December 1949, sensing that the bulk of the population was behind
the CPP, Nkrumah decided to launch a campaign of positive action the
aim of which was to make Britain grant the country the status of a
self-governing territory. By this time the Coussey Constitutional Committee had drafted the new constitution which did not differ much from the
old Burns Constitution. It gave the Governor the same powers he had
possessed under the old political system. Officials appointed in London
by the Secretary of State for Colonial Affairs would continue to head the
ministries of defense and foreign affairs, justice and finance. Commerce
and the mining industry would also be run by the Europeans. The
Legislative Assembly replaced the gubernatorial Legislative Council and
the chiefs held the majority of seats in the new body. The Governor had
the right to veto all decisions taken by the Assembly. As for the main
question – the granting of self-government – the constitution virtually
assumed that the colonial system would remain in place for an indefinite
period. The British government approved the recommendations of the
Coussey Committee and expressed its thanks to the chairman. Now the
Gold Coast's new constitution was to come into force.

This limited constitution provoked a storm of indignation among those
who rallied to the cry "Self-Government Now!". At the initiative of
Nkrumah, who was acting in concert with the Trade Union Congress, the
Ghana People's Representative Assembly was formed. More than fifty
public organizations representing trade unions, the cooperative movement,
youth, women and veterans, with a total membership of over 100,000
took part. A trade unionist, engine driver Pobee Biney, was elected
Assembly Chairman. The colony had never seen anything like it. Only the
chiefs and the UGCC leadership refused to take part in the forum. The
Assembly pronounced the Coussey Constitution unacceptable. On December 15, 1949 *The Accra Evening News* published an article by Nkrumah
entitled "The Era of Positive Action Draws Nigh" in which he delivered
what was in essence an ultimatum to the colonial authorities: if within
two weeks a constituent assembly made up of representatives of the
people elected in direct universal balloting were not convened to draft a
dominion constitution, then a campaign of positive action based on
nonviolence and non-cooperation would be launched throughout the
country.

[1]*Ghana*, pp. 111-112.

In early January 1950 a high-ranking official in the colonial administration, Reginald Saloway, came to the Gold Coast from Britain to meet with Nkrumah. First he tried to intimidate the leader of the CPP by saying that Nkrumah would be responsible for the possible tragic consequences of the upcoming disturbances. When this tack did not work, Saloway, drawing on his many years of experience in India, declared that, in contrast to the Indians, the Africans were not accustomed to suffering and deprivation and that they did not have the staying power needed for a long campaign. Nkrumah stood his ground. Early on the morning of January 8, at the stadium in Accra, he announced the start of positive action which involved strikes, a boycott on British goods, rallies and peaceful demonstrations. Next, he toured the cities along the coast and in the inland districts where the bulk of the Gold Coast workers were concentrated. Here, too, the man who had inspired positive action was given total support.

On January 11 the campaign reached its climax. Trains stopped, offices and stores closed; the Trade Union Congress declared a general strike at enterprises. The economic life of the country was paralyzed. It was the first mass demonstration for national liberation by working people in the history of colonial Africa. The authorities answered it with violence: a state of emergency was declared throughout the country, the army and police broke up demonstrations and destroyed the editorial offices of CPP newspapers. Leaders of the party and trade unions were arrested. Nevertheless, the protest campaign had achieved its main goal. In those few days the political consciousness of the masses had grown significantly. It was now clear that joint action could shake the colonial structure which had heretofore seemed so stable.

The colonial administration dealt harshly with those who had actively participated in the campaign. For incitement to revolt, Kwame Nkrumah was sentenced to three years in James Fort Prison in Accra. He was prepared for this. The bad food and the small cell did not distress him as much as the absence of pencil and paper. In those difficult times it was essential to maintain party unity for future decisive engagements. A few of the Central Committee members who remained at liberty tried to grab the vacant top posts. The newspapers of the UGCC and the colonial administration launched an unprecedented campaign of slander against the members of the CPP and Nkrumah, calling them Communists, subversive elements and hooligans. They predicted that the party would soon disintegrate completely. Then, at long last, Nkrumah received a parcel containing a precious article – a pencil stub. Late at night Nkrumah would lie on the floor of his cell where a narrow shaft of light from the lamp that illuminated the prison yard fell and devise plans for the party's work in the new conditions. In the morning the pieces of paper containing the barely discernible text would be passed to a loyal guard whereupon they were immediately delivered to party headquarters. The people did not forget their leader. On many evenings CPP supporters gathered outside the prison and sang the party anthem for all in the surrounding area to hear. Thus Nkrumah passed his first year in prison.

The Coussey Constitution was approved by the British government and went into force on January 1, 1951. The first general elections to the new Legislative Assembly were set for February 8. On a Sunday morning, in a far corner of the prison yard, a CPP committee discussed a question of great importance: should they participate in the election called for by an unpopular constitution, which the party leadership had continually warned was dangerous, or should they boycott the elections, renounce the parliamentary means of struggle and let the conservative elite come to power, no matter how limited that power was? The majority supported Nkrumah who favored taking part in the election. It was their only chance to continue the struggle for self-government by peaceful means. The party organizations were instructed to put up candidates in every election district. Nkrumah stood in Accra's central district.

Preparations for the campaign began. In his prison cell Nkrumah worked out the party's election manifesto. It was an extensive program promising industrialization, the elimination of unemployment, and democratization of education and health services. The manifesto went on to declare that after independence had been gained, the party would work to create a socialist state in which both men and women would have equal opportunities and where there would be no capitalist exploitation. The manifesto concluded with the call: "Exploited and oppressed Ghanaians, this is your chance to save your country. Vote CPP! ! !"[1]

CPP activists set about the big task of explaining the positions laid down in the manifesto and the party's policies to the masses. Some effort also had to be put into convincing illiterate peasants to go to the polls. They expected no good of the colonialists and in this, the whites' new venture, many of them saw the threat of tax increases. The campaign drew to a close. From start to finish it had been directed from James Fort by Kwame Nkrumah. A leaflet distributed three days before the election

[1]*Great Britain and Ghana,* p. 707.

said of him, "Nkrumah is a man of the common people . . . He is honest, straightforward, hardworking, vigilant, stainless. Through his efforts for Africanization he has encouraged free education, building of roads, railways, harbors and hospitals. We have chosen Nkrumah to lead us toward independence. . . . "[1]

Early on the morning of February 9 the prison authorities informed Nkrumah that he had been elected. Over 98% of the voters in his district had given him their votes. The victories of the other CPP candidates were no less impressive. As a result, 34 of the 38 seats in the Legislative Assembly went to Nkrumah's party. The people of the Gold Coast had voted for independence.

On February 12 Governor Charles Arden-Clarke reluctantly signed the order for the release of Nkrumah and the other CPP leaders. Thousands of people gathered outside the prison to greet their leader. Calls to break down the gate and release the prisoners immediately were heard. At last Nkrumah appeared. For a second there was silence and then it was broken by the sound of shouting and applause. A forest of hands went up in the gesture of welcome used by the members of the CPP. Those who stood in the front rows lifted Nkrumah up onto their shoulders and carried him to an open car. The triumphal procession wended its way to the stadium where two and one half years earlier the formation of the CPP had been announced. The hymn "Lead Kindly Light" was sung. Then Nkrumah went through a ritual purification ceremony. This is how he described it: " . . . the customary expiation was performed by sacrificing a sheep and by stepping with my bare feet in its blood seven times" which was supposed to clean me from the contamination of the prison."[2] As a leader of the people he was obliged to observe the people's traditions. Nkrumah's speech was brief. He thanked the people for all they had done to bring about the release of the CPP leaders and for the warm welcome they had given them. "The struggle continues,"[3] he concluded.

On the following day the Governor invited Nkrumah to his official residence. The African politician had never been inside Christianborg Castle, the majestic white stone fortress with the British flag flying from the main tower. For him it was a symbol of colonial oppression, while the surf that broke over its foundations seemed like the waves of the people's

---

[1] *Ghana and Nkrumah,* ed. by Thomas A. Howell and Jeffery P. Rajasooria, Facts on File, Inc., New York, 1972, p. 12.

[2] *Ghana,* p. 109.

[3] *I Speak of Freedom,* p. 23.

wrath. He had never met Arden-Clarke and the prospect of doing so now made him nervous. The Governor, too, did not expect any good to come of the meeting with the famous "troublemaker."

' This is how Arden-Clarke later described the scene: "That meeting was redolent with mutual suspicion and mistrust. We were like two dogs meeting for the first time, sniffing at each other with hackles half raised trying to decide whether to bite or wag our tails."[1] But this was not just a get-acquainted session. The Governor officially asked Nkrumah, as head of the victorious party, to form a government in accordance with the new constitution. Yesterday's convict had become the head of government affairs. An agreement was reached whereby five of the seven ministerial posts allotted to Africans would go to members of the Convention People's Party. As he left, Nkrumah cast his eyes over the walls of Arden-Clarke's office. From their portraits, the countenances of the Gold Coast's previous governors gazed at him haughtily. Nkrumah sincerely hoped that the collection would expand no further.

This turn of events came as a surprise to the leaders of the UGCC and the chiefs. They had never doubted that their loyalty had earned them the favor of the colonial authorities nor that they were worthy of ministerial portfolios. They were the ones who had drafted the constitution approved by London and the Governor himself had advised them in confidence to get ready for important changes. The fine suits they had ordered from London for official receptions and parties had already been delivered. Their wives had returned from Paris where they had supplemented their wardrobes with elegant French creations. And now, as these men saw it, the British had betrayed them.

Nkrumah did not have any sense of euphoria over the CPP's landslide victory. It was still a colonial government even though the majority of its members were African. At the same time, however, the political situation that had taken shape in the Gold Coast was unique in colonial Africa. Tactical flexibility was vital in order to consolidate this success. At a press conference held immediately after his release from prison Nkrumah declared, "I would like to make it absolutely clear that I am a friend of Britain. I desire for the Gold Coast dominion status within the Commonwealth. We shall remain within the British Commonwealth of Nations. I am not even thinking of a republic."[2]

---

[1]Quoted in F. M. Bourret, *Ghana—the Road to Independence, 1919–1957*, Oxford University Press, London, 1960, p. 177.

[2]*Ghana and Nkrumah*, p. 13.

The results of the Gold Coast elections provoked a broad international response. On the whole, analysts in the West came to the conclusion that this event signalled the beginning of the end of Africa's colonial dependence. At the same time the conclusion of this process seemed a long way off. "It is just 50 years, from the occupation of the interior, since British rule over these territories began; and it is not very bold speculation to believe that they may become fully self-governing nation-states by the end of the century... If the West is to win and hold Africa, the effort needed is thus different from that needed in Asia,"[1] opined the American journal *Foreign Affairs*. The Prime Minister of the racist Union of South Africa, Dr. Malan, was particularly alarmed by the results of the Gold Coast elections. He declared that if other native territories followed this example it would mean "nothing less than the expulsion of white men from practically everywhere between the Union and the Sahara." However he comforted himself with the thought that the Gold Coast "experiment" would undoubtedly fail.[2]

On February 20, 1951 the Legislative Assembly opened. It seemed as though everyone in Accra had come to watch the event. The ceremony was very colorful. The organizers had consciously modelled it on the opening of the British Parliament. The Governor was driven to the hall where the Assembly was to meet in a Rolls-Royce and accompanied by a cavalry escort wearing green and red jackets, seated on black horses and bearing lances. The troops, standing at attention, presented arms. A military band struck up "God Save the King." The organizers had also included local color in their plans. A steady stream of chiefs who were members of the Assembly arrived in expensive cars surrounded by large retinues. Their gold and silverplate crowns, gold necklaces and the gold thread in their sandals shone in the blinding sunlight while their rich clothes were iridescent with all the colors of the rainbow. Kwame Nkrumah and the other members of the CPP leadership who had recently served time in prison somewhat disturbed this symbiosis of Westminster traditions and tribal cults. They made their entrance wearing homemade mortarboards on which the initials of the words "Prison Graduate" could clearly be seen. They were proud of their "prison education" and reminded the colony's real rulers of the Positive Action campaign which, as Nkrumah

---

[1]Margery Perham, "The British Problem in Africa", *Foreign Affairs,* Vol. 29, No. 4, July 1951, pp. 637, 639.
[2]Ibid., p. 642.

declared, could be repeated if the British blocked the establishment of absolute self-government.

One year later the British government was pressured by the inhabitants of the Gold Coast into making an amendment to the constitution in accordance with which Nkrumah began to be called the Prime Minister. With this change his personal prestige and the prestige of the government was raised, particularly in Africa where he became the first Black Prime Minister. This event was widely discussed and inspired a feeling of pride in the Black race. Congratulatory telegrams from abroad poured into government and party headquarters. But the degree to which Africans participated in the governing of the country had not been increased one iota. As before the Governor was in charge of civil administration, the police, army, courts and foreign affairs. Three-quarters of the country's civil servants were British employees of the Colonial Office. Nkrumah realized, however, that this situation could not be preserved long and that there would soon come a time when the Africans themselves would make all the decisions concerning affairs of state. Therefore it was necessary to set about training administration cadres.

Nkrumah made the African ministers who belonged to the CPP turn down the luxurious villas which the "far-sighted" colonial authorities had built for them in Accra's fashionable district. He himself moved into a small two-story detached house in the center of the city and brought his mother from Nkroful to live with him. The ministers and members of the Legislative Assembly who belonged to the CPP were supposed to contribute their relatively high salaries to the CPP fund; in lieu of these they received a fixed payment. Nkrumah was categorically opposed to all contacts between the members of the party who held government office and British officials beyond the walls of governmental institutions. " . . . For what imperialists failed to achieve by strong-arm methods, they might hope to bring off with cocktail parties,"[1] he warned. The lifestyle of the Prime Minister himself was decidedly modest and his days were spent solving numerous urgent problems. An endless stream of ministers, workers, legislators, party activists, women, venders and peasants came from far and near to see him at his home and CPP headquarters. Their requests varied widely. No more than four hours a day could be given over to sleep. Michael Dei-Anang, who worked alongside Nkrumah, recalled that he attended "to official business with care and concern above the ordinary.

[1] *Ghana,* p. 142.

He was a stickler for discipline and hated lazy, slipshod or slovenly work of any kind . . . His working day started long before daybreak . . . "[1]

Nkrumah frequently spoke in the Legislative Assembly, at Party rallies and on the radio. He explained the character of the current stage of the struggle for dominion status, stressed the importance of forming bodies of local self-government to replace the hated district commissioners appointed by the Governor, proposed that an enormous hydroelectric power station be built on the Volta River and that the country be electrified. In addition, he organized a campaign to destroy diseased cacao trees and plant healthy, disease-resistant saplings in their stead. Inexperienced where political stratagems were concerned, the masses expected the Prime Minister and the African government to make rapid and radical changes in their lives. Therefore it was necessary to explain that the government had to act within the narrow confines of the colonial constitution. The country was short of resources and, at times, of simple knowhow and experience. Moreover, British officials frequently sabotaged many of the African government's plans, stirred up anti-government feeling and actively cooperated with the opposition. For these reasons political flexibility was essential. The CPP had to be willing to compromise so as to avoid giving anyone an excuse for provoking conflicts which could complicate the struggle for independence. Nkrumah called the cautious course they followed at that time of hidden confrontation "tactical action."

The situation was further complicated by the negative stand that the influential chiefs took on almost every measure the CPP proposed. They opposed all change not only by virtue of their traditional conservatism but because they were afraid they would be deprived of the privileges the colonialists had granted them. Faithful to the system of "indirect rule," the British preserved almost without change the ancient institution of the chief and relied on it in the conduct of colonial policy. The power the chiefs had over their fellow tribesmen was a very real factor in the political life of the colony. The colonial authorities did not allow chiefs to display independence or dissatisfaction and deposed those whom they found objectionable. On the other hand the chiefs were free to stop any attempts to undermine the foundations of traditional power and tribal structure. Thus, the traditional chiefs were an obstacle to national unity and the liberation movement. In this way an influential group of conformist chiefs was formed who saw a threat to their status in the actions of

[1]Basil Davidson, *Black Star . . .* , p. 97.

young nationalists who came out for equal rights regardless of tribal affiliation, sex or social origin. Admittedly they, too, spoke of independence from time to time but they understood it to mean complete independence of action for the chiefs within the "tribal kingdoms." That is why they resolutely opposed Nkrumah's plans to create a unitary state once independence had been gained.

Especially fervent advocates of a federal state structure were the traditional Ashanti power elite headed by the most influential supreme ruler in the Gold Coast who bore the title "Asantehene." For services rendered to the British, the Asantehene was knighted.

Separatist tendencies were particularly marked in the province of Ashanti. In precolonial times the Ashanti had been on a higher plane of social, economic and cultural development than had the other peoples of the Gold Coast. As far back as the beginning of the 18th century the legendary Ashanti chief Osei Tutu had laid the foundations of a strong centralized state, subjugating many of the neighboring tribes. In the 19th century the Ashanti state became the strongest in West Africa and in the course of several lengthy wars put up a valiant resistance to the British colonialists. The older generation still recalled the events of 1900 when, in answer to the British demand that they hand over the Golden Stool – a sacred symbol of state authority – the people rose up and held off the invaders for a year.

The Ashanti had every reason to take pride in their past but the traditional rulers tried to foster ethnocentric attitudes in them. This local tribal nationalism had socio-economic roots as well. Most of the country's cacao production was based in this area. There was a fairly significant stratum of rich farmers and cacao bean buyers who were satisfied with their situation on the whole and opposed unification with other, poorer regions.

Led by the Asantehene certain members of the most prosperous groups in Ashanti society founded a party with the fine-sounding name, the "National Liberation Movement." Calling for a federal system based on tribal divisions and even for making Ashanti an independent "kingdom" they launched an anti-government campaign. Encountering resistance in the form of Nkrumah's uncompromising position, the Asantehene sent a petition to the Queen asking her to support his demand that the country be partitioned. Nkrumah later wrote, "The raising by the N.L.M. of the demand for federation was eagerly seized upon [by the British] as a hopeful

means of fragmenting our small and largely homogenous country."[1]
And, it can be added, of delaying the granting of independence as long as
possible. The Secretary of State for Colonial Affairs declared that if this
question were not settled by peaceful means the granting of dominion
status would be postponed. The minister's statement touched off a wave
of violence in which members of the CPP in Ashanti were killed and party
organizations were destroyed. Hundreds of Ashanti residents were forced
to flee to other parts of the country. Chiefs who supported CPP policies
were deposed. Nkrumah did not respond to this provocation nor did he
take any repressive measures even though many members of the party's
leadership were strongly in favor of doing so. He believed that serious
disturbances would place the country's future in jeopardy as the Britain
would claim that civil war had broken out in the colony and that it
therefore was impossible to pull out of the country.

The wave of terror reached the capital. One muggy evening when
Nkrumah was out in his veranda there was an explosion. The house was
badly damaged but no one was hurt. This was the first of many attempts
on Nkrumah's life. The reactionary opposition did not differentiate between
political struggle and political murder.

There were other political organizations besides the NLM which opposed
the CPP's centralization policies and profound socio-economic reforms.
In the Northern Territories the Northern People's Party, which called for
the creation of a separate state for the tribes of the North, was formed.
Moslem merchants set up the Moslem Association Party which claimed
to represent the interests of the Gold Coast's 700,000 Moslems. From the
ashes of the United Gold Coast Convention, which had lost all of its
popularity, there arose the Ghana Congress Party. It acted in the interests
of the conservative chiefs and the "old" intelligentsia. There were other,
smaller parties as well. All of these organizations represented the tribal,
regional and religious opposition which fought for its own narrow interests and was incapable of working out any positive program for the
country's development.

In this difficult political climate the Nkrumah government proposed
that important changes be made in the degrading Coussey Constitution;
changes which would in effect abrogate it although they would not bring
about self-government per se. The 104-member Legislative Assembly was
to be directly elected on the basis of universal suffrage. The government
(cabinet of ministers) was to consist exclusively of Africans and take full

[1]*Africa Must Unite*, p. 58.

responsibility for the country's home policy. Defense and foreign affairs would remain the Governor's prerogative. Nkrumah discussed these ideas with the British Conservative government's Secretary of State for the Colonies, Oliver Lyttelton, when the latter visited the Gold Coast in June 1952. Lyttelton agreed to present the proposals to his government if they received the approval of the chiefs and the main political groups. In the end Nkrumah managed to obtain their assent in principle although the chiefs insisted on the creation of an upper chamber in the Legislative Assembly – the House of Chiefs.

The new constitution, called the Nkrumah Constitution, went into force in April 1954. Although it preserved the Gold Coast's colonial status the government was given great leeway in preparing the country for independence. In June the first Legislative Assembly elections under the new constitution were held. The Convention People's Party's campaign slogan, "Forward with Common People", reflected the party's desire to secure the support of the widest possible sections of the population on the question of self-government. The party took the red rooster, representing battle and victory, as its symbol.

On the eve of the elections the right-wing opposition launched a frenzied campaign of slander against the party and its leader, demagogically accusing Nkrumah of neglecting the people's interests and of profit-sharing with the colonists. The British bourgeois newspapers pitched in, too. As Nkrumah later recalled, "all the armory of the British press was brought into play against me and against the Convention People's Party. Special correspondents were sent to discover that we 'were not only Communists, but deep in bribery and corruption'."[1] As a result of this turn of events Party discipline plummeted. Over eighty members of the CPP declared their candidacies for offices for which there were official party candidates. They were therefore expelled from the party. Those who had been expelled immediately joined the opposition.

Despite the machinations of local and international reactionaries, the election results confirmed the people's desire for liberation and their faith in the CPP and its leader. Thousands of people gathered in downtown Accra by an enormous board on which the results of the voting were written in order to hail their party's victory. When Nkrumah appeared in the middle of the night on an improvised rostrum illuminated by spotlights he was greeted by thunderous applause. His party had received

[1] *Africa Must Unite*, p. 57.

72 of the 104 seats in the Legislative Assembly. Of the other official parties the Northern People's Party enjoyed the greatest success, garnering 12 mandates. The rest had to be satisfied with one or two seats each. As it had the majority in the Assembly the CPP formed a government headed by Kwame Nkrumah.

Independence seemed imminent now. But the British were extremely disturbed by the growing radicalization of the liberation movement, by the presence of an influential left wing in it and by the rising popularity of socialist ideas. In order to eliminate political trends which posed a threat to the British, London began to blackmail Nkrumah's government. Nkrumah was given to understand that the activities his party engaged in could be regarded as "Communist." Given the existence of the "cold war" and international tensions this meant being accused of the most terrible "sin" imaginable and that could have far-reaching consequences. A precedent already existed. In 1953 Whitehall had put off granting British Guinea independence indefinitely as it believed that the People's Progressive Party headed by Cheddi Jagan harbored "communist" ideals. British troops went into the country.

Fearing that events in the Gold Coast might take a similar turn Nkrumah was compelled, as head of the government, to sanction a campaign to eradicate "Communist ideas" from the country. He announced in the Legislative Assembly that proven Communists would be ineligible for jobs in government offices, the police and the army. It was declared illegal to bring "communist" literature into the country or to distribute publications from the World Federation of Trade Unions, the World Federation of Democratic Youth and other progressive international organizations. Many trade union leaders who were known for their radical views were dismissed. In this instance Nkrumah acted pragmatically, to a large degree renouncing his convictions in order to achieve his main goal as quickly as possible. True, he was far removed from the communist ideology in his thinking at that time nor did he believe it had any bearing on him. Defining his credo he said, "Today I am a non-denominational Christian and a Marxist socialist and I have not found any contradiction between the two."[1] But it is revealing that Nkrumah does not discuss this aspect of his "tactical action" in his works, particularly in his autobiography where a great deal of attention is paid to the motivation for this or that action. Apparently he realized its ambiguity.

This minor concession to the British, as it may have seemed to Nkrumah,

[1] *Ghana,* p. 12.

had serious consequences for the CPP, as it resulted in the strengthening of the party's right wing. Trends towards bureaucratization of part of the party apparatus and personal enrichment began to develop. The consequences of these negative processes were not then apparent but later they would be revealed in all their unattractiveness and become the cause of many crises within the party and the state.

Meanwhile all of the reactionary opposition groups coalesced around the National Liberation Movement did everything in their power to prevent the attainment of independence on the conditions laid down by the CPP. They devised a federal plan for the future dominion's political structure and presented it to the Governor. Under this plan the key role would be played by the chiefs of four federated regions – the Gold Coast proper, Ashanti, the Northern Territories and Togoland. Kofi Abrefa Busia became the leader of the reactionary forces. Busia's political views were determined to a large extent by his social background and education. Descended from a long line of Ashanti chiefs, he attended Oxford University where he received a scholarship from the Carnegie Endowment, an American philanthropic organization. Appealing to the British government, Busia exclaimed, "We still need you on the Gold Coast ... Your experiment there is not yet complete. Sometimes I wonder why you seem in such a hurry to wash your hands of us."[1] The British were not opposed to seeing these forces head the future independent state and they set a date for new general elections to the Legislative Assembly, hoping that the CPP and Nkrumah would be defeated. They were encouraged in this thinking by the leaders of the opposition who maintained that the majority of the Gold Coast's population was behind them. They also hoped to exploit the fact that Nkrumah's government, which had no real political power and was limited in what it could do, had failed to fulfill the sweeping promises it had made in 1951. The British promised to set a date for the granting of independence after the new elections. In his introduction to the CPP election manifesto Kwame Nkrumah called on all voters to answer two questions as they cast their ballots: " 'Do I want independence in my lifetime?' or 'Do I want to revert to feudalism and imperialism?' "[2]

The voting on June 12 and 17 was peaceful despite provocative acts by members of the opposition and the openly malevolent campaign that had been conducted by the British press. The people of the Gold Coast once

[1]*Ghana*, p. 279.
[2]*Revolutionary Path*, p. 119.

again demonstrated their faith in the Convention People's Party and voted for independence and a single, unified state. Nkrumah's party captured 71 of the 104 seats in the Assembly. Even in Ashanti where the NLM enjoyed the greatest support the CPP received 43% of the votes. Britain's attempt to use the opposition organizations to split the national liberation movement had not been successful.

At long last it was announced that on March 6, 1957 the British colony of the Gold Coast would disappear from the political map of Africa and in its place would appear the sovereign state of Ghana. Kwame Nkrumah could not help but have a sense of legitimate pride. Born in the years when the formation of the colonial system in his country was being completed, he had witnessed its crisis and soon he would watch it break up completely. Moreover, he had participated directly in that process. Acting within the framework of the peculiar "diarchy" his government had managed to accomplish a great deal in the areas of education and health care, and it had raised the population's living standards. Tuition fees for primary education had been abolished. The number of children enrolled in school had doubled. The network of secondary schools and teachers' training colleges had been significantly expanded. The campaign to wipe out illiteracy among adults was well underway. Literature was being created and newspapers were being published in local languages. Between 1951 and 1957 nine new hospitals had been built and fifteen had been modernized; greater attention had been given to expanding medical services in the backward Northern Territories. Kwame Nkrumah wrote about all this in his autobiography, which also contained these ardent words by the Soviet writer Nikolai Ostrovsky, words which were deeply imprinted in Nkrumah's heart: "Man's dearest possession is life, and since it is given him to live but once, he must so live as not to be besmeared with the shame of a cowardly existence and trivial past, so live that dying he might say: all my life and all my strength were given to the finest cause in the world – the liberation of mankind."[1]

At the beginning of March numerous delegations from every continent began to arrive in Accra to take part in the festivities on the occasion of the declaration of the country's independence. Britain was represented by the Duchess of Kent. The Soviet delegation delivered to the Speaker of the Legislative Assembly a message from the USSR Supreme Soviet expressing the latter's desire to establish direct ties with Ghana's parliament.

[1]*Ghana,* p. 206.

At a reception in the Ambassador Hotel, which had been built especially for this purpose, Kwame Nkrumah, addressed the delegates from 56 countries: "We are most anxious to establish friendly and cordial relations with all countries and we hope that it may be possible for us to play our full part in the United Nations, whose official representatives we are honored to have among us."[1]

On March 6, 1957, exactly one hundred and thirteen years after the British signed the first inequitable treaty with the Fanti chiefs setting the stage for colonial penetration into the Gold Coast, the ceremonial declaration of Ghana's independence took place. Dressed for the occasion in their national costumes, more than 100,000 men, women and children, most of whom had travelled on foot to the capital from every corner of the land, witnessed the stirring ceremony. At the stroke of midnight the British Union Jack was lowered and a fresh ocean breeze lifted the tricolored flag of Ghana for all to see. Its red stripe symbolized the blood that had been shed for liberty and the glory of those who had fought for independence. The yellow stripe symbolized the abundant gold which lay in the country's depths, the country's well-being. The green stripe symbolized cacao and the wealth of the tropical forests. The large black five-pointed star in the center was the symbol of the African people's unity in the struggle against colonialism. Then the band struck up the national anthem. The last notes of the song were drowned by the cries, "Freedom! Freedom!" People laughed and wept and hugged one another.

Then Nkrumah began to speak. "At long last the battle has ended! And thus Ghana, your beloved country, is free forever. And here again, I want to take the opportunity to thank the chiefs and people of this country, the youth, the farmers, the women, who have so nobly fought and won this battle. Also I want to thank the valiant ex-servicemen who have so cooperated with me in this mighty task of freeing our country from foreign rule and imperialism!... We must realize that from now on we are no more a colonial but a free and independent people! But also, as I pointed out, that entails hard work... We know we are going to have a difficult beginning but again I am relying upon your support, I am relying upon your hard work, seeing you here in your thousands, however far my eye goes... Today, from now on, there is a new African in the world and that new African is ready to fight his own battle and show that after all the black man is capable of managing his own affairs. We are going to

[1] *I Speak of Freedom,* p. 95.

demonstrate to the world, to the other nations, young as we are, that we are prepared to lay our own foundation."[1]

For a long time afterwards African drums continued to resound in the damp night air, hailing the birth of the independent state in their ancient language. They were echoed by the victorious people singing their proud new song:

> *Land of our birth we pledge to thee,*
> *Our love and toil in the years to be;*
> *As we are grown to take our place*
> *As men and women with our race.*
>
> *Land of our birth, our faith, our pride,*
> *For whose dear sake our fathers died;*
> *Oh Motherland we pledge to thee,*
> *Head, heart and hands in the years to be.*[2]

Black Africa was stepping into the forefront of world history.

[1] *I Speak of Freedom,* pp. 106–107.
[2] Ibid., p. 47.

V. Searching for Paths of Development

The long-awaited independence celebrations had come to an end. Now the wind was sweeping crumpled leaflets, posters and multicolored streamers into piles on the streets of Accra. The foreign VIPs had departed for the four corners of the earth and the inhabitants of Ghana's cities and villages had left the capital. Life began its normal round.

Little remained of Nkrumah's recent sense of elation and optimism or of his thirst for contact with crowds of thousands. It would be wrong to say that he was not prepared to do the day-to-day work necessary to bring about the country's independent development, work not likely to give instantaneous results. Moreover, he repeatedly reminded the party and the people that a long and difficult road lay ahead. But during the struggle for Ghana's liberation Nkrumah and the party he headed had not had a well-defined program for the country's economic and political development. Even though the CPP program adopted in 1951 indicated that the party had as its goal the building of a socialist state where there would be no place for capitalist exploitation, serious thought had not been given to the methods that would enable it to realize this goal. Like an incantation, Nkrumah's oft repeated slogan, "Seek ye first the political kingdom and all things shall be added unto you" had exercised a spellbinding effect not only on Nkrumah's audiences but on him as well. Now the question was unavoidable: what would be "added unto" them?

Thus far, very little had been. At the time it gained independence, Ghana had a typically colonial economy, characterized by extreme backwardness and a one-crop agricultural system. Oriented towards meeting Britain's needs, it was completely dependent on the world capitalist market. Cacao represented over 70 percent of the country's total exports. Industrial diamonds, gold, manganese, bauxite and timber made up the balance. Almost all of this was shipped to Britain.

Even though the Gold Coast economy had been relatively well developed compared with those of other African colonies, the country was almost totally lacking in industry. Those few Africans who had capital were unable to invest it in manufacturing industry as the British colonialists strove to keep that market to themselves. Local capital had access only to retail commerce, the construction industry and a few spheres of the mining industry. On the eve of independence the colony's economy was characterized by its small scale. The Gold Coast was a land of petty merchants, artisans and craftsmen. Factory-based industry, as yet in embryo, was represented by a brewery, a soap factory, a tobacco factory, a soft-drink factory and several garment factories. This for the entire country! All of the necessary manufactured goods right down to handkerchiefs and matches were imported from Britain.

The main branch of the economy was agriculture, which was backward and based on a communal land tenure system that still bore the marks of patriarchal feudalism. These factors lay at the root of the low marketability of the country's agricultural goods. The British encouraged the production of cacao beans alone; the other branches of agriculture were neglected. A country blessed with an abundance of natural resources, it nevertheless had to import potatoes, cauliflower, carrots, beetroot, milk, butter and much more from Britain.

Nor did the machinery of state Ghana inherited from the colonialists satisfy the needs of the newly independent nation. Moreover, the British did everything in their power to complicate the work of the sovereign state's apparatus during the first and most difficult stage of its operation. A few days after the independence day celebrations, Nkrumah and the members of his government went to the former residence of the British Governor, Christianborg Castle, in order to set up their offices and take over the business of running the country. They were greeted by empty rooms, bare walls and bits of broken furniture. Everything down to the last scrap of paper had been sent to Britain. This unequivocal act showed that the belief that the former colonial ruler would play a positive role in the development of independent Ghana had been an illusion.

Nkrumah sized up the situation in Ghana after the colonialists left: "It was when they had gone and we were faced with the stark realities, as in Ghana on the morrow of our independence, that the destitution of the land after long years of colonial rule was brought sharply home to us. There were slums and squalor in our towns, superstitions and ancient rites in our villages. All over the country, great tracts of open land lay untilled and uninhabited, while nutritional diseases were rife among our people. Our roads were meager, our railways short. There was much ignorance and few skills. Over eighty percent of our people were illiterate, and our existing schools were fed on imperialist pap, completely unrelated to our background and our needs. Trade and commerce were controlled, directed and run almost entirely by Europeans."[1]

It was imperative that the leaders of Ghana set about to determine the path of development, and work out a program of socio-economic reform and its theoretical foundation.

There are two political-economic systems in the world. However, Nkrumah supposed at that time that Africa did not need to choose between them. Rather, it had to search for a system of its own which would make use of "the best that capitalism and socialism had to offer". It would be based on traditional communal institutions, on the cooperation and egalitarian principles of distribution which had once characterized them. This symbiosis would be made possible by "African socialism", whose special quality and difference from Marxism-Leninism was emphasized in every possible way.

It was thought that the material-technical base and social structures of this type of "socialism" could be created through "economic democracy." This reformist idea was earnestly promoted by European Social-Democrats during the period preceding African independence. In the postwar years the Labourites had more than enough opportunities to spread the ideas of Labourite democratic socialism in Britain's colonies. But it would perhaps be incorrect to say that the ideological influence of the social reformists was the sole reason for the decided popularity these ideas enjoyed in the African countries during their first years of independence. A kind of "reciprocal interest," also existed. For those African ideologists who saw socialism not as a goal, but rather as a means of transforming society and who conceived of the path to socialism as the implementation of reforms that would not affect the roots of society, these ideas were the most acceptable.

The influence reformist ideas had on Kwame Nkrumah at that time is reflected in the way he defined the aims of Ghana's independent development. "These aims," he wrote, "embrace the creation of a welfare state based upon African socialist principles, adapted to suit Ghanaian conditions, in which all citizens, regardless of class, tribe, color or creed, shall have equal opportunity..."[2]

[1]*Africa Must Unite,* p. xiii.
[2]*I Speak of Freedom,* p. 163.

Like many other African revolutionaries who assumed power in young states, Kwame Nkrumah saw the "adaptation" of socialism to the urgent tasks of the African revolution as his mission. He believed that in its "pure form" scientific socialism was only applicable to the West. African reality, it seemed, confirmed his view. Society had not yet been rent by the conflict of class interests and the main antagonistic classes – the proletariat and the bourgeoisie – were in embryo. In the years immediately following the achievement of independence, the unity of the social forces that had fought for national liberation continued to be preserved to some extent. It seemed that a basic postulate of Marxism – the principle of the universal class struggle – did not work in Africa. As for the doctrine of the dictatorship of the proletariat, young national-democratic ideologists, influenced by European Social-Democrats, maintained that it had arisen in conditions specific to Russia alone. Thus, for example, George Padmore, who had a considerable impact on Nkrumah's thinking, wrote that the difference between "Russian" and "African" socialism was that the latter was not dictatorial by nature. African socialism, he added, should be based on Western principles of democratic socialism.

It must not be forgotten that the African states came into being and chose their orientation at the height of the cold war unleashed on the socialist system by imperialism. For some time a few leaders of young African states feared that by making an unequivocal choice in favor of socialism they would be damaging their neutral stance as well as jeopardizing their chances for economic aid from the Western countries when African states were almost totally dependent on the world capitalist market.

As "African socialism" was becoming a means of bringing about postcolonial society's development, it was first and foremost in need of an economic foundation. Kwame Nkrumah had never been particularly interested in economics. Nor, for that matter, had the majority of his colleagues. During the first two years of independence the Prime Minister's economic advisor was Arthur Lewis, a liberal British professor of economics and a native of the West Indies. Until 1961 Ghana's economic policies were based on the principles Lewis laid down. In essence they were that the government should not participate directly in production. Instead, it should limit itself to assisting private capital in whose hands the productive sphere of the economy should be. As the Ghanian private sector was weak this meant that foreign capital was to serve as the main instrument of economic development. However, this did not occur even though Nkrumah called on the Western countries to implement a plan for Ghana along the lines of the Marshall Plan for postwar Western Europe. Apparently he was deluded as to the motives of the Americans for granting "aid" and its consequences.

Despite the substantial benefits and guarantees given foreign investors the influx of capital to Ghanian industry was insignificant. Conditions in Ghana did not promise large profits in the sphere of industry. Not only did the "economic liberalism" policy not produce a high rate of economic growth but it led to an enormous foreign trade deficit and a sharp decrease in foreign currency reserves.

The question of working out a new economic program based on different principles was placed on Ghana's agenda. The experience he had gained while governing the newly independent state and the loss of illusions he had suffered concerning the "good intentions" of the imperialist countries led Nkrumah at the beginning of the 1960s to the conclusion that reformist development concepts were inoperable. "If... we are to fulfil our pledge to the people and achieve the program set out above," he declared, "socialism is our only alternative."[1] A conscious choice in favor of the socialist orientation was made. Later events were to confirm that the choice had been correct – 1961 became a turning point in the country's history.

In the same year Nkrumah made an official visit to the Soviet Union at the invitation of the Presidium of the USSR Supreme Soviet and the USSR Council of Ministers. On July 10 he arrived in Moscow at the head of a delegation which included ministers, top party officials and members of Parliament. The Ghanian delegation was met at the airport by Soviet leaders who saluted them "as representatives of a freedom-loving African country with which we are successfully developing relations of lasting friendship and close cooperation, as representatives of a people actively fighting to eradicate colonialism once and for all and to strengthen peace and friendship among all nations."[2] The guests wanted to get as detailed a picture as possible of life in the country of triumphant socialism so the schedule of their two-week visit was quite full.

In Moscow Kwame Nkrumah held talks with Soviet leaders, visited the Lenin Mausoleum; Ball-Bearing Plant No. 1; Moscow University, where he was awarded an honorary doctorate; and the USSR Academy of Sciences. He toured the Exhibition of Economic Achievements, travelled down the

[1]*Africa Must Unite,* p. 119.
[2]*Pravda,* July 11, 1961.

Moscow Canal, acquainted himself with the progress of housing construction in the capital's Southwest district, and attended the theater and circus.

The Ghanian delegation's stay in Moscow was followed by a trip to Irkutsk Region, to Uzbekistan, the Ukraine and Leningrad. Particularly memorable was the stop in Siberia, an area known for its inhospitable cold and impassable taiga. To their amazement the members of the delegation found that this vast region had become a major industrial area and a huge construction site where Soviet men and women from a wide variety of ethnic groups enthusiastically worked. Siberia's future was even more exciting, as the Ghanian leaders learned when they acquainted themselves with the construction of the Irkutsk and Bratsk hydroelectric power stations. Speaking in Irkutsk, Nkrumah said that the delegation had come to the USSR, to use Lenin's words, to "learn, learn and learn". They wished to learn how the Soviet Union had succeeded in becoming industrialized in such a short time and how it had achieved the political unification of its various ethnic groups.

Next the delegation boarded an IL-18 and flew to colorful Uzbekistan – a land with an ancient and original culture which had marched into the 20th century during the years of Soviet government. They toured cotton plantations and a dairy farm and met agriculturists. In honor of the distinguished guests a party was given at the Kzyl Uzbekistan Collective Farm. There the Ghanians had an opportunity to evaluate the Uzbek saying, "Receive guests better than you would your father". Wearing a *tyubeteyka* (a traditional Uzbek cap) Kwame Nkrumah entered the ring of collective farmers and, to the general delight began to dance to ancient Uzbek rhythms.

The exotic was just a supplement to the serious business of studying various aspects of the socialist system, the foundations of which Nkrumah wished to lay in Ghana. He was interested literally in everything: from the system of economic planning to relations within the family. In speaking of the impressions he had gained during his visit, Kwame Nkrumah declared that what the delegation had seen in the Soviet Union had been extremely instructive. Mentioning in particular the cohesion and friendship of the fifteen constituent republics of the Soviet Union he stressed that their example was an inspiration to the peoples of Africa who should unite in the struggle to liberate the continent from colonialists, neo-colonialists, and racists. In speaking of the African countries' prospects for economic development the President noted that electrification was their first priority. To electrify all of Africa was, in Nkrumah's words, to "Leninize" it.[1]

The Ghanian delegation's visit to the USSR was crowned by a mass meeting of friendship between the peoples of the Soviet Union and the Republic of Ghana held on July 24 in Moscow. Speaking at the meeting, Nkrumah said that wherever he had gone he had been greatly impressed by the industriousness and enthusiasm of the Russians and the energy with which they did their work. He added that the delegation would take back with them pleasant memories of the peaceable and friendly Soviet people.[2]

At the time, i.e. at the start of the 1960s, Kwame Nkrumah became convinced that the institutions of bourgeois democracy were inapplicable to any African state that was carrying out profound socio-economic reforms. The 1957 constitution, drafted and foisted on the country by the British, proclaimed Ghana to be a sovereign state with a cabinet and parliamentary system of government like that in the United Kingdom.

During the first years of independence Nkrumah himself supposed that bourgeois democracy was a system of government which could be employed in African conditions. He wrote, "Having placed our faith in the working of a liberal democracy, I ardently desired to give it every chance ... "[3] However, he soon realized that imposing an alien political system on a traditional set of social ties was not only ineffective but was fraught with danger for any state which had chosen the path of progress.

In November 1957 all of the opposition parties founded on tribal, regional or religious principles merged and became the United Party. The party and its leader, Kofi A. Busia, concentrated all their efforts on opposing national consolidation and the centralization of state power. The opposition came out against all the measures taken by the national government whether they concerned the formulation of a progressive foreign policy or the development of education and health care. At the same time the opposition did not have any sort of positive program to offer. Not limiting itself to its customary methods of struggle – lies, slander and bribery – it began committing acts of violence. In November 1958, 43 active members of the United Party were arrested and charged with working to overthrow the government. Not long before a prominent member of the opposition had purchased military equipment in London

---

[1]See: *Azia i Afrika segodnya*, No. 11, 1961.

[2]*Pravda*, July 25, 1961.

[3]*Africa Must Unite*, p. 73.

under a false name and tried to have it delivered to the borders of Ghana. At the start of the following year a plot on Nkrumah's life was uncovered. Once again, the conspiracy was traced back to the opposition. Busia left the country and emigrated to Europe where he continued his subversive work.

In the wake of these events Kwame Nkrumah became convinced that bourgeois political "pluralism" was both inapplicable and dangerous in the context of a young independent state. He came to the conclusion that the existence of a reactionary opposition only served the purposes of imperialism which gave it moral and material support so that it could hold the process of revolutionary change in check. Nkrumah commented, "It has been the unfortunate experience in all colonial countries where the national awakening has crystallized into a popular movement seeking the fundamental democratic right to the rule of majority, that vested interests have come to the aid of minority separatist groups ... In fledgeling states, imperialist interests flourish where there is an atmosphere of dissention. They are endangered in an atmosphere of national unity and stability."[1]

How the country should be governed was an important issue in post-colonial Ghana. After independence was gained the state remained a dominion in the British Commonwealth whose sovereign was the British Queen. The head of state, who was appointed by the Queen, was the Governor-General. The Earl of Listowel took Arden-Clarke's place. In addition, he was named Commander-in-Chief of Ghana's armed forces while the Chief of Staff was the British general, H. T. Alexander. The members of the national government had to swear allegiance to the British crown.

This state of affairs seriously encroached upon Ghana's sovereignty and made it difficult for the country to pursue independent domestic and foreign policies. A movement sprang up involving the trade unions and other mass organizations of working men and women demanding that Ghana be made a republic. However, it was not so easy to take this step. The British Conservatives had foreseen this turn of events and insisted that a special clause be included in the 1957 Constitution in accordance with which any change in that document would have to be approved not only by Parliament but by councils of tribal chiefs as well. They correctly assumed that the traditional rulers would perceive a threat to their privileges in the republican form of government. The well-known Soviet

[1] *Africa Must Unite*, pp. 75-76.

Africanist I. I. Potekhin related the following typical story which illus-trates this point. A few months after independence was achieved, an Indian shopkeeper hung a mat with the legend "The Republic of Ghana" near the gate to his shop. One must suppose that this was the result of an error in the shopkeeper's reasoning: he had apparently decided that Ghana, like India, could be considered a republic. This incident triggered a chorus of protests from the feudal elite. The mouthpiece of the reaction-ary opposition, the *Ashanti Pioneer,* published a photograph of the mat and asked whether this did not reflect the mood of the governing party. Perhaps Nkrumah's government planned to introduce a republican sys-tem like India's to Ghana? The reactionary papers tried to make a scandal out of the incident. The chiefs demanded an explanation from Nkrumah. They were told that the government did not have anything to do with the Indian shopkeeper's initiative but that if a republic were to be proclaimed it would not signify the abolition of the institution of tribal chiefs.[1] The furor died down but it was clear that the tribal elite would oppose a transition to a republican system.

Nevertheless, relying on the support of the people, Kwame Nkrumah initiated the struggle to have the constitution, so degrading to national dignity, reconsidered. In 1958 the Ghanian Parliament approved a bill submitted by the Prime Minister which gave that body the right to amend the constitution. This cleared the way for the institution of a republican system. The opposition voted against the bill.

In February 1960 a government-sponsored law was passed vesting Parliament with the functions of a constituent assembly and granting it the right to draft the constitution for a republic. The reactionary opposi-tion accused Nkrumah of "rebelling" against Elizabeth II. For their part they put forward a ridiculous proposal under which Ghana would become an "elective monarchy" headed by one of the traditional chiefs. The English reactionary press took up these charges and launched a campaign of slander against Nkrumah, accusing him of violating democratic prin-ciples and aspiring to become a dictator.

In April a referendum was held on changing the country's system of government. At that time the electors were also asked to vote for the candidate whom they wished to see become Ghana's first President. The Convention People's Party nominated Kwame Nkrumah. The United Party

[1]See I. I. Potekhin, *Gana segodnya* (Ghana Today), Geografgiz, Moscow, 1959.

urged Ghanians to vote against the republic but with their usual inconsistency they declared that J. B. Danquah was their candidate for President.

Nkrumah was well acquainted with the unscrupulous methods employed by the opposition. In order to avoid being accused of rigging the referendum and presidential elections he called upon the African countries and members of the British Commonwealth to send observers to Ghana. Approximately 90 per cent of the electors cast their votes for the republic and Kwame Nkrumah as its President. The republic's constitution declared all of the legislative and executive acts which had limited Ghana's sovereignty void. It also laid the legal foundation for creating a unitary state, the only viable type of state system in the case of an African country which brings various ethnic groups together within its borders.

On the evening of July 1, 1960 the ceremonial proclamation of the republic took place. The president of Guinea, Sékou Touré, and W. E. B. Du Bois were given places of honor among the more than 500 foreign guests who attended the ceremony. When darkness had fallen, Nkrumah walked up to a tall pedestal topped by a round bowl. One second later a flame burst forth within it, a flame symbolizing the people's unquenchable desire for liberty. Bells rang, the ships in the harbor sounded their sirens, people in the streets hailed the birth of the Republic of Ghana with cries and songs. The country's first President took the following oath: "I, Kwame Nkrumah, do solemnly swear that I will well and truly exercise the functions of the high office of President of Ghana, that I will bear true faith and allegiance to Ghana, that I will preserve and defend the constitution, and that I will do right to all manner of people according to law without fear or favor, affection or ill will. So help me God."[1]

In accordance with the new constitution Nkrumah became not only the head of state but the chief executive, the head of government. He was also made commander-in-chief. Now he had the legal and political base he needed to set a course for the progressive transformation of society.

Kwame Nkrumah's duties were not extended on paper alone. He did all the work each post entailed from start to finish and relied little on his assistants. This necessitated extraordinarily tight scheduling and a high level of organization. The President's working day began very early. Rising at four a.m. he did calisthenics. This was usually followed by a game of tennis. Before breakfast he dictated letters. After nine there were meetings with officials, diplomats, journalists, and ordinary citizens who came

[1] *I Speak of Freedom,* p. 235.

to him with their problems and requests. Three p.m. signalled the start of a short break. Sometime after five Nkrumah was back at his desk. In the time that remained before he went to bed he wrote speeches, articles and books. He was an avid and speedy reader. His office and apartment were filled with books on a wide range of topics in history, philosophy, culture and economics. Sometimes he even came to official meetings, book in hand, and shared his impressions of what he had read with those present. The President tried to foster a love of reading in everyone. Not infrequently he gave books to ministers and civil servants and asked them to write summaries of the works, ostensibly because he needed them in his work.

On particularly busy days when he was too fatigued to continue working Nkrumah would go into the reception room and engage in yoga. A visitor who happened by at that moment could see the nation's President standing on his head. Ten minutes sufficed to reinvigorate him. All those who knew Kwame Nkrumah well commented on his amazing capacity for work. He was in a hurry to do as much as possible towards realizing his ideas. "I must go on," he frequently said. "Time is against me."[1]

Nkrumah believed that only by disciplining the mind and body could one work effectively. To this end he fasted every Friday even though his normal diet was anything but rich: palm-nut soup, fruit, vegetables and juices. Periodically Nkrumah went into seclusion at his modest beach house near Half Assini where, like his hero Mahatma Gandhi, he spent several days fasting and meditating. Putting aside all of his daily cares he relaxed and brought his mind to a state of absorption and concentration.

Nkrumah did not partake of alcoholic beverages. When it was necessary to propose a toast at official receptions, he made himself take a sip of champagne. The President shunned invitations to the various parties his associates gave. Not just because he was a teetotaler. The festive and carefree atmosphere that reigned there annoyed him. " . . . He would say, wryly: 'No wonder we can't unite Africa! You all consider independence as just one long cocktail party.' "[2] Nkrumah worked and tried to inculcate a taste for work in others. But far from everyone in the corridors of power followed his advice. Revelling in their new status, they tried to live as merrily and "elegantly" as possible.

At the same time Kwame Nkrumah was not a somber ascetic. Easy and interesting to talk to, he quickly established contact with people and

---

[1]Genoveva Marais, *Kwame Nkrumah: As I Knew Him,* p. 19.
[2]Ibid., p. 21.

knew how to win them over. This is how I. I. Potekhin described the impression the President made on him during their meeting: "Nkrumah is a short, wonderfully built middle-aged man, dressed in the European manner. An intelligent, strong-willed face, a friendly smile, a soft, pleasant voice, lively eyes that twinkle with laughter – everything about this man helped dispel completely the tension that marked the first few minutes of our meeting."[1] He was a witty man who enjoyed and appreciated a joke. Obliged to spend the greater part of his day alone at his desk, he occasionally called one or another of his friends and asked him or her to tell him a funny story. Having laughed, if it really was funny, he got back down to work. Among his hobbies, in addition to tennis and reading, Nkrumah enjoyed swimming, horseback riding, chess and gardening. He devoted a considerable portion of his free time to the breeding of roses. Ordering literature on the subject, he soon became an expert, but his main hobby was music. Nkrumah surrounded himself only with the things he needed and one of these was a record player. On Sundays he could listen to classical recordings for hours on end. His favorite pieces were *The Creation* by Haydn and *The Messiah* by Handel. This music roused him, distracted him from the cares of the preceding week and gave him a new burst of energy.

On his free days Nkrumah could give more time to his family. At the end of the year that had ushered in Ghana's independence, Nkrumah married a twenty-seven-year-old Egyptian woman, Fathia Helen Ritzk. The young couple met for the first time at the wedding, a fact which gives Nkrumah's biographers grounds on which to assert that the marriage was political in nature and was aimed at consolidating Ghana's ties with the largest and most influential country in Arab Africa. Nasser congratulated the newlyweds and sent them gifts. However the wedding itself in Accra was modest. The guests were Nkrumah's mother, a few of his closest friends and the bride's uncle. The ceremony was performed in accordance with the canons of the Greek Orthodox Church. In terms of religious affiliation, Fathia's family were Copts – Egyptian Christians.

All who knew Nkrumah's wife spoke of her calm, composed nature. Ghana's First Lady did not like official receptions or parties and preferred to seclude herself in her small apartment in Christianborg Castle which had been renamed Osu Castle. Her children were her primary concern. One year after the Nkrumahs were married their first child was born. He was named Gamal in honor of Nasser. Next they had a daughter, Samia,

[1] I. I. Potekhin, op. cit., p. 116.

and then a son, Sekou, who was named after Nkrumah's friend and the President of Guinea, Sékou Touré.

Nkrumah loved his children and when he was with them he forgot everything else. Everything except his work. That is why he could not be with his youngsters regularly or for longer periods. He had even less time for his hobbies. After the path of development had been determined, all his time and energy were taken up by his efforts to develop the bases of a progressive political course and their theoretical foundation.

VI. Nkrumahism: the Theory

In the period that Kwame Nkrumah was head of state his socio-political, economic and philosophical views were systematized to some degree. The anti-imperialist mood which had characterized the period of struggle for independence was replaced by a militant anti-imperialism; pan-Africanism became more progressive and began to be perceived as a movement for one united Africa which would countervail imperialism; ideas concerning social equality, drawn from various sources, were molded into the theory of a "national type" of socialism. These changes indicate the main directions of Nkrumah's spiritual and political development. It is in independent Ghana that the theoretical foundation of the ideological concept which came to be called Nkrumahism in political literature was fully laid. The most important components of this theory were anti-imperialism, pan-Africanism and socialism. The views Nkrumah held on ideology and theory while he was in office are set forth in his articles, speeches, and above all in such works as *I Speak of Freedom; Africa Must Unite; Neo-Colonialism: The Last Stage of Imperialism; Consciencism: Philosophy and Ideology for Decolonization and Development with Particular Reference to the African Revolution.*

Anti-imperialism.

The national liberation movement in Africa is part of the global struggle against imperialism. The success of the anti-colonial movement on the African continent showed that Lenin was right in believing that most of the earth's population would eventually join in the struggle against all forms of oppression and for the economic, social and spiritual emancipation of peoples everywhere.

At the end of the 1950s and start of the 1960s, when the African countries had just been liberated from colonial dependence, many African politicians were uncertain as to the kind of relations the young sovereign states would have with their recent colonial masters. In an attempt to maintain their standing in the African countries, yesterday's colonial powers went to great lengths to show Africans the need for their paternal care and an interdependent foreign policy. The former British colonies found themselves within the British Commonwealth of Nations while the former French colonies (with the exception of Guinea) all became members of the Franco-African Community. This new type of subjugation was strengthened by the network of economic, political and military agreements that were thrust upon the young states. To many in Africa it seemed that once sovereignty was attained, exploitation by the imperialist powers would be impossible while the traditional links between the colonies and the imperialist countries would be transformed. Moreover, the African countries counted on receiving substantial economic aid from the former Colonial rulers. In 1958 Nkrumah said, " ... The evolving forms of the Commonwealth is an institution which can work profoundly for peace and international cooperation."[1]

The events that followed the liberation of the African countries demonstrated that the imperialist powers did not have altruistic reasons for providing them with aid and that imperialist "aid" and "cooperation" signified economic, political and ideological penetration of the African countries. By the early 1960s Kwame Nkrumah was writing, "Imperialism is still a most powerful force to be reckoned with in Africa. It controls our economies. It operates on a worldwide scale in combinations of many different kinds: economic, political, cultural, educational, military; and through intelligence and information services. In the context of the new independence mounting in Africa, it has begun, and will continue, to assume new forms and subtler disguises."[2]

During the initial years of the African states' independent development the imperialist powers attempted to remain entrenched in the economies of these countries, using methods to achieve this end which differed little from those they had employed in colonial times. The former ruling countries and other imperialist states strove to keep the liberated countries in the position of agro-raw material appendages and as far as possible to preserve the colonial structure of their economies. By the mid-1960s the methods employed in pursuing neocolonialism's economic policies

---

[1]Ali A. Mazuri, *Towards a Pax Africana,* Weidenfeld and Nicolson, London, 1967, p. 72.
[2]*Africa Must Unite,* p. xvi.

had changed substantially. To a large degree this was brought about by the existence and growth of the economic and political might of world socialism, giving the African countries an opportunity to reorient their economic ties and develop them on the basis of fundamentally different types of relations. In addition, the scientific-technological revolution, the economic rivalry among capitalist states, and the growing specialization and cooperation of production made the former methods of exploiting developing countries ineffective. The imperialist powers adapted to the changing times. They went from opposing the economic growth of the former colonies to assisting the development of a few industries there. They were particularly careful to monitor the socio-economic development process in each newly free country and keep them within capitalism's orbit. In order to meet this aim, African states were provided with economic and financial "aid." In the 1960s, as today, by no means all countries were favored with imperialist "charity." The greater part of this "aid" went to those states whose governments had attuned their economic systems to capitalism and established close political ties with their "benefactors."

Kwame Nkrumah emphasized that, in contrast to the aid socialist states provide, aid that advances the industrialization of the developing countries, Western "aid" primarily goes towards developing the infrastructure essential for the further exploitation of these countries by imperialist monopolies. Nkrumah deserves credit for being among the first in Africa to understand the mechanism by which this "aid" operates. Imperialist aid, he said, "must, in fact, come out of the trading profits made from forcing down the prices of primary products bought from the African countries and raising the cost of the finished goods they are obliged to take in exchange"[1] and "is used for the exploitation rather than for the development of the less developed parts of the world."[2] Nkrumah's conclusions became particularly relevant during the struggle that grew up in the '70s and '80s for a review of the inequitable economic relations that exist between the imperialist states and the developing countries, for the establishment of a new world economic order, for "economic decolonialization."

As a result of the neocolonialist policy pursued in regard to the African

[1]*Africa Must Unite*, p. 182.

[2]Kwame Nkrumah. *Neocolonialism: The Last Stage of Imperialism,* International Publishers, New York, 1965, p. x.

countries some of them were integrated into the European Economic Community's activities. This policy was designed to prevent young states from embarking on the path of non-capitalist development and to keep the main means of actively influencing the character and direction of the former colonies' socio-economic development in the hands of monopolies. Kwame Nkrumah strongly opposed attempts to make Africa an "associate" of the Common Market. Terming the actions of the European Economic Community a policy of collective imperialism, Nkrumah alerted the African countries to the danger of economic enslavement. He wrote, "The overseas associated members have gone in as providers of raw materials, not as equals dealing with equals... Nor could there be any idea of solid industrialized advancement for these African states in the interests of their people."[1] The neocolonialism of the Common Market, Nkrumah explained, "is a 'heads I win, tails you lose' policy, which aims to create a bitter schism among the independent African states or else to cajole them all into the fold of the European market, in the same old imperialist relationship of the European rider on the African horse."[2] Kwame Nkrumah warned that if the African states joined that closed imperialist association it would not only lead to the strengthening of their economic dependence but would also threaten their political autonomy. And as the EEC was closely linked to NATO they would, to a certain extent, have to renounce the policy of non-alignment and desist in their active support for the national liberation movement on the African continent. "In short," he bluntly concluded, "they will have sold their African birthright for a mess of neo-colonialist pottage."[3] Later events proved the accuracy of Nkrumah's prediction. By offering the "associated" African nations a few privileges the European capitalist powers gained a new opportunity to influence the policies these countries pursued. Today many African politicians realize that "association" with Western Europe is based on discrimination, inequality and neo-colonialism. The African countries now strive to establish new types of economic ties with the European states, ties that will further their own development.

The danger of growing economic pressure on independent Africa prompted Kwame Nkrumah to search for new ways of neutralizing attempts to

[1]*Africa Must Unite*, pp. 160, 162.
[2]Ibid., p. 161.
[3]Ibid., p. 162.

enslave it. Nkrumah believed that close economic cooperation among the newly free nations was essential if Africa's independent economic development was to be assured. "In the face of the forces that are combining to reinforce neocolonialism in Africa," he wrote, "it is imperative that the leaders should begin now to seek the best and quickest means by which we can collectivize our economic resources and produce an integrated plan for their careful deployment for our mutual benefit."[1] Nkrumah believed that in order to accomplish this the African countries should join together, first, in a number of economic communities, and then in a single African common market. This would help avoid competition among the African states, pool their resources and coordinate economic policy. As experience has since shown this was, on the whole, a fairly realistic program for cooperation, totally realizable and acceptable to the newly free nations. The majority of African countries are working towards broadening intracontinental cooperation and trade links and setting up regional economic associations. In addition, increasing support is being given to the idea of setting up an African economic community by the year 2000. This idea is contained in a declaration adopted by the 14th session of the Organization of African Unity in 1977.

Political and ideological expansion by neo-colonialism poses no less a threat to Africa than economic penetration does. This distinction is, however, highly theoretical given that the economic, ideological and political aims of neo-colonialism are tightly interwoven and interdependent. At a time when the accent is being shifted from national to social liberation, when socialist ideas are becoming increasingly popular around the world and when some countries are spurning the capitalist path of development, the imperialist powers attach great significance to the political and ideological influence they have over developing countries. The forms of this influence and methods by which it is effected differ and change as the political situation on the African continent changes.

When they exited from Africa, the colonial powers fixed the boundaries of the future independent states as they saw fit in an attempt to create a series of sovereign states that would continue to be dependent on the former colonialist countries due to their economic backwardness and domestic instability. Nkrumah called this neocolonialist policy "political Balkanisation". "Neo-colonialism," he wrote, "is based upon the principle of breaking up former large united colonial territories into a number of

[1]Ibid., p. 172.

small non-viable states which are incapable of independent development and must rely upon the former imperialist power for defence and even internal security."[1] Striving to secure political influence, the imperialist powers thrust political and military cooperation agreements on the African states. These agreements enabled them to involve the newly independent countries in military-political alliances, to set up military bases on the continent and to remain entrenched in these states.

The "Balkanisation" of the African continent was fraught with the danger of border disputes and armed clashes between independent states. Unfortunately, this carefully thought out neo-colonialist policy bore fruit. Nkrumah noted that some leaders continued to squabble with their neighbors and became the victims of nationalist sentiments – all beneficial to their enemies. It is imperialism's nature to consciously exaggerate national, tribal and religious differences.

In a few African countries the colonial powers succeeded in handing power over to pro-imperialist circles and comprador bourgeois groups while suppressing the more radical trends within the national liberation movement. The leaders of these countries were completely satisfied with the independence they had received and local, narrow nationalistic interests began to prevail over national and African interests. This, Nkrumah noted, had led to capitulation to the neo-colonialists and to a nationalism founded on dimwitted and aggressive chauvinism.

Against those states that pursue independent domestic and foreign policies, imperialism employs the strategy of coups and the physical liquidation of their leaders. Nkrumah noted that as the struggle to determine a path of development mounted, Africa experienced a series of coups and assassinations inspired by the imperialist powers, which disposed of the best leaders of the young nation-states. Nor does imperialism hesitate to intervene directly in African countries not wishing to bow to imperialist diktat. Nkrumah declared that the imperialist powers had adopted the strategy of "limited wars" and added that they were occasionally able to secure a decisive result "by landing a few thousand marines or by financing a mercenary force ... "[2] The events that followed in Angola, Benin, Chad, the Comoro Islands, the Seychelles and other African countries as well as in Afghanistan, Lebanon, Nicaragua and Grenada have shown that imperialism is increasingly giving priority to armed intervention in the

[1]Kwame Nkrumah, *Neocolonialism: The Last Stage of Imperialism*, p. xiii.
[2]*Neocolonialism: ... ,* p. xi.

affairs of sovereign developing nations as it pursues its neo-colonialist policies.

When ultra-conservative, reactionary forces came to power in the U.S., a concentrated attack on the liberation movement was begun under the guise of combatting "international terrorism." Subversive activities were stepped up, particularly against those states which had embarked on the revolutionary path of struggle for social and economic progress. The ruling circles in the United States regard this type of adventurist policy as a direct continuation of the global struggle between the capitalist and socialist worlds. That which Nkrumah had noted as a tendency now appears to be the main strategic theme of U.S. imperialism's policies as they pertain to the socialist-oriented countries. And that is understandable. The achievements of progressive states, their ever increasing role in world politics and, finally, their steady growth in number clearly indicate the general, scientifically based prospects for the newly free nations' development. This provokes increasing alarm and animosity in imperialist circles. "It is because the socialist orientation demonstrates its viability that imperialism attacks it so bitterly," noted B. N. Ponomarev.[1]

Western policies aimed at maintaining racist regimes in southern Africa became an important means of exerting pressure on independent Africa. Kwame Nkrumah's stance on the colonial-racist regimes that threatened the independence and sovereignty of all African countries was consistent and uncompromising. Ghana initiated a boycott of South Africa, a boycott which received the support of all the African countries. Concerted action by the independent nations of Africa led to the political and economic isolation of the racist Pretoria regime on the continent. In 1965 when the Southern Rhodesian racists declared "independence" Nkrumah called on the African countries to take decisive action up to and including the use of force, against the government of Ian Smith. The government of Ghana broke off diplomatic relations with Britain, which had connived with the racists. Kwame Nkrumah exposed the colonial and racist policies the Western powers, principally the United States, pursued with regard to the national liberation movement in the southern part of the continent. He maintained that since American money was used to recruit mercenaries in Southern Rhodesia and South Africa it was impossible to convince Africans that the United States was not interested in seeing racism return to Africa. Later events in southern Africa demonstrated that Nkrumah had

[1] *Pravda,* October 21, 1980.

been right. While the U.S. was still trying to dissociate itself, if only in words, from the inhuman policy of apartheid in the 60's, since the '70s and particularly since the early '80s the aggressive Washington-Pretoria axis has steadily grown in strength. The United States persistently works to consolidate the position of its strategic ally, South Africa, and, hence, its own position in the southern part of the continent. The U.S. also does everything in its power to weaken national liberation movements and progressive regimes in the region.

The ideological subversion the imperialist powers carry out in Africa has become a form of neo-colonial expansion. These activities include the dissemination of the bourgeois value system, the activities of religious organizations, control of the mass media, the retention of the key positions in the educational system and much more. Particular vigor in this area is displayed by the U.S. which, for historical reasons, did not initially have as much political or ideological influence in Africa as did Britain or France. By the start of the 1960s, immediately following the national liberation of most of the African countries, more than 600 missionary, educational, philanthropic and other private and government-sponsored U.S. organizations were at work in Africa. "Dating from the end of 1961, the U.S. has actively developed a huge ideological plan for invading and utilizing all its facilities from press and radio to Peace Corps,"[1] Nkrumah warned the African public.

Anti-communism is one of neocolonialism's ideological weapons. "Alongside the battle for imperialist supremacy," Nkrumah wrote, "there wages the fight against the ideological camp of socialism, into which the warring imperialists make an all-out effort to trail the developing countries... In this way the anti-communist campaign is used to further imperialist aims."[2] He went on to say that another goal of this campaign is to prevent the developing countries from making their choice in favor of socialism. Nkrumah regarded the USSR and the other socialist states as the African countries' natural allies and the decisive force in the struggle against imperialism. He declared that if it had not been for the Soviet Union, the movement to free Africa from the colonial yoke would have felt the full force of brutal and harsh oppression.[3]

[1]Kwame Nkrumah, *Neocolonialism:...*, p. 247.
[2]Ibid., pp. 54–55.
[3]See *Pravda,* July 25, 1961.

In order to keep the developing countries from embarking on the only true path of development, the imperialist states try to spread reformist ideas within the national liberation movement. This tactic is not new. In 1920 Lenin said that "the imperialist bourgeoisie is doing everything in its power to implant a reformist movement among the oppressed nations, too."[1] An analysis of these policies, carefully camouflaged in pseudo-socialist phraseology, led Nkrumah to the conclusion that imperialism operates in Africa "through labor arms like the Social-Democratic parties of Europe... and through such instruments as the International Confederation of Free Trade Unions (ICFTU)..."[2] Present-day social-democracy aspires to convert the ideologists of young independent states, warp their understanding of the ideas of scientific socialism, foist the concept of "democratic socialism" on them and sow distrust towards the policies of the socialist countries. In recent years these efforts have increased in scale and degree of organization. In 1981 eleven social-reformist and pro-bourgeois parties came together to form the African Socialist International (ASI). The organizers of the ASI have not given up trying to expand this association by drawing in the revolutionary democratic parties of the continent in the hope that they, too, will degenerate to reformism.

For the developing countries an effective means of opposing imperialist neo-colonialist policies is the policy of neutralism and non-alignment. The African countries were first drawn into international politics at the time of the "cold war," which was launched by the imperialist powers. The Western countries tried to involve the new states in aggressive anti-socialist blocs and set up military bases on their territories. However, imperialism did not succeed in making the African states part of its political system. The majority of them prefer to speak and act for themselves on the international scene as they justifiably fear that close political alliance with the Western powers could lead to the reestablishment of the latter's domination and the spread of neo-colonialism. Non-alignment has become one of the most important components of the African states' foreign policies. However, not all of the African countries which have declared their support for the principles of non-alignment and neutralism

---

[1] V. I. Lenin, "The Second Congress of the Communist International, July 19-August 7, 1920. Report of the Commission on the National and the Colonial Questions, July 26", *Collected Works,* Vol. 31, Progress Publishers, Moscow, 1982, p. 242.

[2] Kwame Nkrumah, *Neocolonialism: ...*, p. 244.

see them as anti-imperialist principles. Some leaders believe that, being non-aligned, their countries no longer need to get involved in such important international issues as disarmament, the struggle for peace or the condemnation of imperialist and colonial wars. They regard non-alignment as the preservation of their "neutrality" in all that does not directly affect their countries. Kwame Nkrumah called this "negative neutralism." It was, he added, "completely impotent and even dangerous."[1]

At the same time, however, Nkrumah combined a clear grasp of the principles of neutralism with a belief that Africa should play the role of a "third force" in international relations. This error stemmed from an incomplete understanding of the nature of the ideological confrontation between the capitalist and socialist systems and from a perception of the "cold war" as a struggle between the great powers for supremacy in international relations. This kind of political position was fairly widespread during the first years of the African states' independence even among progressive politicians and ideologists. Many of them believed that in order to pursue an independent foreign policy the East and the West had to be treated in the same manner. Nkrumah was of the opinion that Ghana should follow a middle course maintaining the balance between East and West. "I really believe in a Third Force,"[2] he said.

Equating the peaceable policies of the Soviet Union and the other socialist countries with the aggressive, imperialist policies of the United States and its allies, and advocating that an "equal distance" be maintained from the world of socialism and the world of capitalism makes it significantly more difficult to realize the anti-imperialist potential of the African non-aligned movement and creates false notions concerning the aims of the aid and support the socialist countries provide independent Africa. Some African countries have followed a pragmatic course which in essence has consisted of not overtly displaying their sympathies or antipathies to either the East or the West and receiving aid from both. Besides these pragmatic motives there have been "romantic" motives as well behind the "third force" policy. Kwame Nkrumah was an exponent of these. He was of the opinion that Africa, with its inherent belief in fairness and equality, should play the role of mediator in the East-West conflict. "We may not have arms, but there is something like moral force," said the President of Ghana, who thought that it would make "a distinctive

---

[1] *Africa Must Unite*, p. 200.
[2] *I Speak of Freedom*, p. 36.

African contribution to international discussions and the achievement of world peace."[1]

However, with time Nkrumah's belief in the "third force" policy was supplemented by a more precise understanding of the nature of the contradictions between socialism and capitalism. In order to resist imperialist "diktat" Nkrumah thought that the African countries should adhere to the policy of positive neutralism. "Our slogan is 'Positive Neutrality'. This is our contribution to international peace and world progress,"[2] he wrote. To Nkrumah's mind this type of neutralism presupposed not an amorphous pacifism but an active struggle against imperialism and colonialism together with practical action in the struggle for peace and disarmament. Credit for working out the principles of "positive neutrality" does not go to Kwame Nkrumah. They were first formulated by Nehru shortly before the 1955 Bandung Conference. Nevertheless Nkrumah did a great deal to bring about their realization in Africa, interpret them and give them a pointedly anti-imperialist quality. After the 1961 Belgrade Conference of the leaders of neutralist countries, Nkrumah, Nehru, Sukarno, Nasser and Tito were rightfully considered the fathers of the non-aligned movement which now encompasses the overwhelming majority of newly independent nations and is having greater and greater influence on world politics. Given the rising level of international tension since the start of the '80s, and the escalation of the arms race touched off by the U.S., the struggle for peace and detente has become most pressing.

Kwame Nkrumah devoted the greater part of his theoretical works to an analysis of the modern methods of imperialist exploitation – neocolonialism. From his writings it is clear that already in the early '60s he had fully recognized its danger. He was one of the first in Africa to do so. Moreover, his analysis of this phenomenon almost completely corresponded to those made by Marxist scholars. By examining the policies of the former colonialist countries and their imperialist allies as they were pursued in new conditions Nkrumah was able to draw profound conclusions, the majority of which have not lost their relevance today and are widely shared by the progressive forces of Africa. These conclusions are also significant because they constitute the first instance in which an African ideologist and politician exposed imperialism.

---

[1]Quoted in: W. Scott Thompson, *Ghana's Foreign Policy 1957–1966. Diplomacy, Ideology, and the New State,* Princeton University Press, Princeton, N.J., 1969, pp. 35, XI.
[2]*I Speak of Freedom,* p. 219.

On the whole Kwame Nkrumah saw anti-imperialism as a policy to be actively pursued by the African countries in order to achieve economic liberation and strengthen their political independence. It should, he thought, resolutely counter attempts by the imperialist powers to keep the newly free nations in the position of agricultural raw material appendages, to foist economic and political controls on them, to forbid ties with the socialist countries, and to realize their aggressive aspirations that threaten peace throughout the world.

Pan-Africanism.

One of the most important tasks the ideology of the African national liberation movement must accomplish is substantiating the ways in which unity may be achieved among the continent's anti-imperialist forces. The idea of African unity, which arose from the pan-African movement, was the basis for many of the concepts of national liberation. At first some of the adherents of this idea thought that unity of action in the struggle against the common enemy – colonialism – would inevitably lead to the destruction of the colonial borders so alien to the Africans, and to the creation of a single African state. This conviction was reflected, for example, in the decisions of the Fifth Pan-African Congress. After the majority of African countries gained independence, the conceptions of pan-African unity were honed, and the forms they took changed but the essence remained the same – Africa's unity was absolutely necessary if the struggle for the political, economic and spiritual decolonialization of its peoples was to continue.

Kwame Nkrumah was one of the most active and consistent champions of the idea of an anti-imperialist union of Africa's peoples and states. He made no small contribution toward bringing this union about. A significant portion of his time and energy was devoted to developing the theoretical and practical foundations on which African unity would be built once the continent had been liberated.

Nkrumah is best known as the author and advocate of the idea of forming a single African state that would embrace the entire continent. He saw the realization of this idea as the key to accomplishing all the tasks which face the African revolution – the struggle against imperialism and neo-colonialism, the liquidation of economic and cultural backwardness, the overcoming of tribalism. Moreover, he thought of this union not as a distant prospect but as an immediate goal, the order of the day. In *Africa Must Unite* Nkrumah wrote that "the continental union of Africa is an inescapable desideratum. Here is a challenge which destiny has thrown out to the leaders of Africa. It is for us to grasp what is a golden opportunity to prove that the genius of African people can surmount the separatist tendencies in sovereign nationhood by coming together speedily, for the sake of Africa's greater glory and infinite well-being, into a Union of African States."[1]

Nkrumah's certainty that such a union could be achieved was based on the tenets of pan-Africanism which affirmed that the Africans form a single national community and that the elimination of the artificial colonial boundaries would lead to creation of a single African state. He tried not to notice that after the countries of Tropical Africa had acquired their sovereignty, pan-African nationalism was replaced by a narrow, country-oriented nationalism. The young states had only just begun to taste the fruits of the independence they had sacrificed so much to gain and they jealously guarded their sovereignty – the primary and tangible result of their struggle. Moreover, the lengthy period of subjugation had given rise to significant socio-economic and cultural-political differences among the African countries.

The idea of creating a Union of African States of the sort envisioned by Nkrumah did not find support among the majority of African countries. Some national leaders – Nasser, Modibo Keita and M. Milton Obote – thought this step premature while others – Félix Houphouet-Boigny, Habib Bourguiba and Leopold Senghor – were opposed on principle but claimed that they did not support the idea because such a union would be difficult to create. Some politicians thought that Nkrumah had just one goal in mind – to establish Ghana's hegemony in Africa and satisfy his personal ambitions.

It is hard not to agree that the idea of the United States of Africa, as put forward by Nkrumah, was unrealistic. The accomplishment of a task as difficult as that of uniting the young nation-states with their variegated ethnic compositions under a single government requires not so much that certain leaders desire it as that the peoples themselves strive for unification. Although Nkrumah maintained that the masses "spontaneously understand and uphold the need for African union"[2] this was no more than a case of wishful thinking. The obstacles to the creation of a single

[1]*Africa Must Unite,* pp. 221-22.
[2]Ibid., p. 193.

state embracing the entire continent were obvious. Neither the economic nor the social prerequisites existed in Africa then, nor do they now. As far as the accusations concerning Nkrumah's hegemonic aspirations are concerned, they appear to have been groundless. The main objective of his struggle was the creation of a union of African states which would countervail against world imperialism. Nkrumah declared more than once that he was ready to work for the good of Africa under the leadership of anyone who was capable of unifying the continent; although, naturally, he did not exclude the possibility that he himself could head the future pan-African continental government.

One of the main factors complicating the creation of a political union was the existence of a class-related and ideological delimitation of the African states. A reflection of the confrontation of socialism and capitalism around the world, there appeared in Africa groups of countries that chose differing paths of development and conceptualized the social aspect of African unity in a variety of ways.

Nkrumah recognized these difficulties, too. But he believed that they could be overcome within the framework of a single state. Not content to limit himself to theoretical considerations of African unification, Nkrumah took steps towards bringing it about. On May 1, 1959 during Nkrumah's visit to Conakry, it was announced that Ghana and Guinea had formed the Union of African States. The document setting forth the basic principles of this union specified that the two countries would coordinate their foreign policies while retaining the main attributes of their sovereignty. The citizens of the two countries had, in addition to citizenship in their respective countries, citizenship in the Union. It was agreed that economic policy would be closely coordinated and a common bank of issue would be established. Guinea, which found itself in a difficult position after refusing to join de Gaulle's Franco-African Community, received an impressive loan from Ghana even though Ghana itself was in desperate need of foreign currency at that time. It was now clear that Nkrumah had been sincere when he repeatedly declared that he would devote all of Ghana's resources to the cause of achieving African unity.

The Republic of the Congo was to have become the third member of the Union. During a brief visit to Accra in early August 1960, Premier Patrice Lumumba signed an agreement with Nkrumah under which the newly formed state was to join the Union of African States. Plans called for the creation of a federal government, an integrated foreign policy and coordinated action in the fields of economic planning and defense. Leopoldville was to have become the capital of the Union. In September, however, Lumumba was removed from office and later murdered. The plan was fated not to be realized.

Nevertheless, a third black star soon appeared on the red, gold and green flag of the Union of African States. In 1961 the Republic of Mali joined the Union. The Union Charter adopted on July 1, 1961, stipulated that concerted action should be taken in the fields of diplomacy, economics, culture and science. The guiding principles of the Union of African States were proclaimed to be the destruction of colonialism in any shape or form, and the strengthening and development of ties of friendship and cooperation among the countries of Africa. The union of Ghana, Guinea and Mali was an active and viable association, erected on an anti-imperialist foundation. Despite the difficulties caused both by the fact that the members of the Union did not have common borders and by the leaders' differences of opinion on several questions, this union played a positive role in the cause of bringing Africa together by influencing the formation of future pan-African organizations and the consolidation of Africa's progressive forces.

The necessity of unity of action among the African nations, a theme Kwame Nkrumah returned to again and again, became even clearer in the early '60s. As a result of the African revolution's increasingly profound social content and attempts by imperialism to effect a split in the national liberation movement, political groups began to appear in Africa who defined their tasks on the African and world scene in a variety of ways. The Casablanca Group brought together Ghana, Guinea, Mali, the United Arab Republic and a few other states on a solidly anti-imperialist basis. At the same time twelve African states – former French colonies – formed the moderate-to-conservative Brazzaville Group which was later renamed the Monrovia Group after being joined by several English-speaking countries and North African states. In this instance, the main danger consisted in the fact that certain Western circles, propagating the reactionary political idea of Euro-Africanism, had participated in the creation of this bloc. The Casablanca and Monrovia groups took diametrically opposed stands on the most burning issues in Africa at that time – the Congolese crisis and the Algerian people's struggle against French colonialism.

A split within Africa, imperialism's attempts to expand its influence as well as to limit and even liquidate the hard-won gains of the African revolution, conflicts among African states – in light of these events African politicians began to realize that Africa could not remain disunited without exposing itself to danger. More and more people took up the call for African unity although these two words were interpreted in a variety of ways, ranging from the creation of a single African state such as Nkrumah proposed to the idea put forward by the Liberian president, William Tubman, that a purely formal association which would not place its members under any obligation be set up along the lines of the Organization of American States. The search for a mutually acceptable solution to the problem of unifying the African countries was brought to a successful conclusion. In May 1963 representatives of thirty-one of the continent's states signed the Charter of African Unity in Addis Ababa. Thereby the Organization of African Unity (OAU) was formed.

On the occasion of the OAU's foundation Kwame Nkrumah published *Africa Must Unite.* There he once again fervently stressed the need for Africa's political and economic integration and for the creation of a continental government. The day before the OAU was formed he once again called on the African heads of states to come together in an African union, emphasising that "no single African state is large or powerful enough to stand on its own against unbridled imperialist exploitation."[1] But the resolution had already been drafted. Nkrumah was acquainted with it in substance and did not conceal his disappointment. The grandiose idea that had possessed him since his university days had not been realized and the pan-African ideal which he had hoped to see achieved during his lifetime became more distant than it had been before Africa's liberation.

The Charter of African Unity was a compromise reflecting, on the one hand, the point of view of the revolutionary-democratic forces who tackled the problem of African unity in a radical way and, on the other, the opinion of a large group of countries that took a "moderate" stand. The OAU was not intended to be a tight-knit political association; however, the progressive leaders and Nkrumah personally did the organization a great service by ensuring that it was founded on the principles of anti-colonialism, anti-imperialism and positive neutralism. The founding of the OAU became a milestone in the history of the African national liberation movement.

Even after the meeting in Addis Ababa Nkrumah did not give up the idea of creating a United States of Africa. Rather, he began to look for a way of forming a union using the mechanism of the OAU. He hoped that joint action to solve common problems on the part of the member countries would increase their mutual understanding and help smooth

[1] *Ghana and Nkrumah*, p. 95.

over political differences which, in turn, would facilitate the creation of a single African state. "I considered the establishment of the OAU," Nkrumah said, "as an important step forward from which we had quickly to move on to the formation of a Union Government of Africa."[1]

The period of "great expectations" passed quickly and the OAU encountered serious difficulties. At first these were primarily related to intervention by hostile external forces. Having been forced to retreat in Africa, imperialism attempted to regain lost ground in the early '60s. Kwame Nkrumah put forward the idea of creating within the framework of the OAU joint armed forces and a joint command to defend the gains of the African revolution and bring about Africa's final liberation from colonialism and racism. Speaking to the heads of the OAU member states at a Conference in Cairo in 1964 he called on those assembled to approve the idea of creating a Union Government of Africa and a Joint African High Command in principle, at the very minimum, if they could not adopt an immediate resolution to this effect.[2] Once again Nkrumah's proposal did not receive the backing of the majority; it was supported to a certain degree by Nasser and Touré.

The last OAU meeting Nkrumah attended took place in 1965 in the capital of Ghana. He tried to impart to the meeting the properties of an outstanding political event signifying a new stage in the movement for African unity. The streets of Accra were decorated with OAU flags and the portraits of 36 heads of African states. A complex of buildings was erected for the meeting at a cost of six million pounds sterling. Late into the night Nkrumah tried to convince his colleagues of the need to adopt his new proposal on uniting the African countries while maintaining the sovereignty of each. But once again he encountered either open or covert resistance from most of the delegates. In the form its Charter had given it, the OAU seemed to represent the most acceptable embodiment of the idea of African unity. The OAU never returned to this question again. Nkrumah's idea for a pan-African state has proved unacceptable in present-day African conditions. The African countries are now working to strengthen their national state systems and broaden intra-African economic, political and cultural ties. Nevertheless, this does not diminish the large, positive contribution Kwame Nkrumah made to the cause of strengthening African unity and giving it an anti-imperialist orientation.

Nkrumah's struggle to create some type of continental state union was

---

[1]Quoted in: Oginga Odinga, *Not Yet Uhuru*, Heinemann, London, 1967, p. xv.

[2]See *Revolutionary Path*, p. 296.

just one aspect of his multifaceted work to organize the actions of all the revolutionary forces in Africa. The triumph of the anti-colonial revolution in Ghana was of exceptionally great significance for the continuing struggle to liberate Africa and determined its role in the African people's national liberation movement. Under Nkrumah's leadership Ghana became the main galvanizing force behind the movement for Africa's anti-colonial and anti-imperialist unity, while his name became a symbol of hope in the most diverse parts of the continent. This was facilitated by the fact that the liquidation of colonialism in Africa was proclaimed to be the primary goal of the new state. Speaking at an Independence Day celebration Nkrumah declared, "We have done with the battle and we again rededicate ourselves in the struggle to emancipate other countries in Africa, for our independence is meaningless unless it is linked up with the total liberation of the African continent."[1] The events that followed demonstrated Nkrumah spoke these words in earnest.

In April 1958, one year after independence was achieved, Accra hosted the first Conference of Independent African States. This is how Kwame Nkrumah defined its goals in a speech delivered at the opening of the conference: "We are here to know ourselves and to exchange views on matters of common interest; to explore ways and means of consolidating and safeguarding our hard-won independence; to strengthen the economic and cultural ties between our countries; to find workable arrangements for helping our brothers still languishing under colonial rule; to examine the central problem which dominates the world today, namely the problem of how to secure peace."[2]

It should be noted that this was the first occasion when representatives of North and Tropical Africa – Ghana, Ethiopia, Liberia, Sudan, the United Arab Republic, Lebanon, Tunisia and Morocco – met to discuss African problems. "Today we are one. If in the past the Sahara divided us, now it unites us,"[3] the Ghanian leader declared to the conference. Kwame Nkrumah regarded the African continent as an organic whole and attached great significance to establishing close ties with the Arab countries of Africa. To this end he began to give a good deal of his attention to the problems of the Middle East which the Arab states had a vital interest in seeing resolved. During his visit to the U.S. in July 1958 Nkrumah presented

---

[1] *I Speak of Freedom,* p. 107.
[2] *Revolutionary Path,* p. 128.
[3] Ibid., p. 129.

President Eisenhower with a set of proposals designed to bring peace to this explosive region. The U.S. Congress had already approved the so-called Eisenhower Doctrine which laid the groundwork for a long line of military adventures by Washington in the Middle East. A sharp rise in American imperialism's colonialist machinations took place. At that time the Arab East had not yet been named "an area of vital U.S. interest"; attempts to subordinate Arab states were justified by the need to "defend" them from a mythical aggressor. The demagogic nature of American "concern" for the safety of this region was obvious to Nkrumah. His proposals included the substitution of U.N. troops for U.S. forces in Lebanon, international guarantees of Lebanon's neutrality and a guarantee from the great powers that they would respect and ensure the sovereignty of every country in the Middle East. The White House did not react in any way to these proposals but the prestige Ghana's Prime Minister enjoyed rose noticeably within Arab political circles. Nkrumah's policies with regard to Algeria also promoted the establishment of closer ties with the North African countries. His government was one of the first to recognize the Republic of Algeria's provisional government and at the time when this recognition was most needed. Bowing to pressure from France, most of the former French colonies did not support the Algerian people's struggle for autonomy.

In December 1958 the Nkrumah government took the initiative and organized the All-African People's Conference, the first pan-African conference of opponents of colonialism and imperialism. Such outstanding figures in the national liberation movement as Julius Nyerere, Felix Roland Moumié, M. Milton Obote, Patrice Lumumba and Kenneth Kaunda attended. A historic slogan was put forward on that occasion – liberate all of Africa in this generation's lifetime. The methods used to achieve this goal, it was noted in one of the conference's resolutions, could vary, be violent or nonviolent, and should be determined by the prevailing situation.

The All-African People's Conference had a great impact on the national liberation movement in Africa. This was reflected in the surge in the anti-colonial struggle which occurred in various parts of the continent at that time. Africa's foes noted this as well. Western imperialist circles began accusing Nkrumah of pushing the colonial population onto the road of violence and illegal acts. Responding to these allegations Nkrumah declared: "There are many people in and outside Africa who attribute the recent disturbances in Nyasaland, in the Congo and in other colonial territories of Africa directly to the deliberations which took place at the

All-African People's Conference held in Accra. Such people believe that Ghana has become the centre of anti-colonial forces and political agitation for independence in Africa... On our part, I wish to say that this accusation is perhaps the greatest tribute that the enemies of African freedom could pay to Ghana. If, indeed, the attainment of independence by Ghana, or the attendance at conferences in Ghana by youth from other parts of Africa has proved the spark of inspiration for nationalist action in the several African territories, then this is a situation of which we can justly be proud. In this regard, I wish to say in clear and unmistakable terms that Ghana has no apologies to render to anybody; nor have we any excuses to make."[1]

Ghana truly had become a focal point for all of the anti-imperialist, anti-colonial forces on the continent. At Kwame Nkrumah's initiative the Bureau of African Affairs was created to study the question of African unity. This organization took the place of the special advisor on African affairs, a post held for two years by George Padmore, who died in 1959. The Bureau did a great deal to popularize the idea of African unity. Its English and French language publications found their way to all of the countries in Africa. Ghana did not just provide diplomatic and moral assistance to those African peoples who were working to wipe out colonial regimes and create nation-states. Many of those who took up arms to free the last colonial territories received their training in Ghana. It should be added that citizens of a few independent African countries who opposed the conservative policies of their governments also received military training in Ghana. This greatly complicated Nkrumah's relations with the leaders of these states. Thus, for example, when it became known in 1965 that the next OAU meeting would be held in Ghana, the governments of Niger, Upper Volta, Ivory Coast, Dahomey and Togo announced that they would not participate unless Ghana ceased providing military training to their citizens.

Nkrumah had a great influence among the younger leaders of the national liberation movement and he tried to support them in every way he could. Patrice Lumumba was an ardent supporter of Nkrumah, shared many of his views and turned to him for advice. From the time of their meeting during the All-African People's Conference, Lumumba was an ardent supporter of African unity as envisioned by Nkrumah. Another consistent opponent of imperialism, Oginga Odinga, wrote, "My convic-

---

[1]Kwame Nkrumah, *I Speak of Freedom*, p. 198.

tion that African unity had to be unbreakable had been reinforced by my talks with Kwame Nkrumah."[1]

Nkrumah regarded the struggle for African unity as part of the universal movement for peace, disarmament and the triumph of the principles of peaceful coexistence. Only peace, he asserted, could ensure the African countries' independent development and further strengthen both their state systems and their economic and social progress. "The balance of forces in the world today has reached such a stage that the only avenue open to mankind is peaceful coexistence," wrote Ghana's President. "The alternative to this is chaos, destruction and annihilation."[2] Nkrumah believed that a united Africa could make an important contribution to the cause of peace and progress for mankind. "World peace today," he wrote, "needs Africa's total independence, needs Africa's unity, as positive contributions to an elimination of the elements engaged in creating the conditions for war."[3]

Nkrumah constantly came out against the retention of old military bases and the construction of new ones on the African continent. He also opposed Africa's transformation into a nuclear test site for the imperialist powers. On those occasions when he did not receive backing on these questions from the leaders of certain African countries he tried to appeal directly to the people, calling on them to take collective action to oppose the involvement of Africa in the military policies of the imperialist powers. He contended that it should be based on the principle of "non-violent positive action." Nkrumah envisioned peace marches in the vicinity of military bases and areas where the French planned to test nuclear devices with the aim of disrupting the testing. Admittedly, attempts to carry out acts of this kind did not meet with particular success. In December 1959, for example, representatives of several countries, led by Michael Scott, a South African priest, set out from Ghana for a French nuclear testing site in the Sahara which they hoped to penetrate but they were stopped by French troops in Upper Volta the following month. Nevertheless, this action drew the attention of the world public to the dangerous and insulting African policy French imperialism pursued. The government of Ghana sent a strong protest to France declaring that there was no land in Africa which "belonged" to the European powers and that the African

[1]Oginga Odinga, *Not Yet Uhuru*, p. 165.
[2]*Africa Must Unite*, pp. 203-204.
[3]Ibid., p. 203.

peoples would not allow atomic explosions to occur on their continent. In the early '60s Kwame Nkrumah proposed that Africa be declared a nuclear-free zone. His call is particularly relevant today, when certain imperialist circles are encouraging the racist South African regime to act on its desire to use nuclear weapons as an instrument of political blackmail against those independent states of Africa opposed to colonialism and racism in the south of the continent.

The work Kwame Nkrumah did in the interests of peace and the progress of mankind gained international recognition. In 1962 the President of Ghana was awarded the International Lenin Peace Prize. The resolution of the committee awarding the International Lenin Prizes "For the Promotion of Peace Among Nations", signed by Academician Dmitri Skobeltsyn, Louis Aragon, John D. Bernal, Renato Guttuso, Pablo Neruda and others, noted his "outstanding service to the cause of preserving and strengthening peace"[1]. The other prize winners that year were the French artist Pablo Picasso, the Pakistani poet Faiz Ahmad Faiz, the Hungarian statesman Instrván Dobi and the Chilean activist Olga Poblete de Espinosa. Nkrumah valued this award highly and emphasized more than once that having received it he was duty-bound to work continuously to decrease the international tension caused by the actions of imperialism.

Kwame Nkrumah made an important contribution to the development of the idea of anti-imperialist unity in Africa, the realization of which he linked to democratic reforms in the newly free nations of the continent. The theoretical and practical work Kwame Nkrumah did in the interests of the African continent's unity is to a large degree still relevant today. Strengthening the African countries' anti-imperialist unity has become even more urgent in connection with the processes by which the social substance of the national liberation movement in Africa is made more profound.

Socialism.

The wide currency the idea of socialism gained in the national liberation movement zone is a result of the deepening of capitalism's general crisis, brought on by the triumph of the Great October Socialist Revolution. Those who take part in the anti-imperialist struggle sooner or later come to the conclusion that capitalism is a system which does not meet the

[1] *Pravda,* May 1, 1962.

needs of the peoples of Africa. The anti-capitalist temper of the masses is reflected in the political and ideological doctrines of many states on this continent.

Kwame Nkrumah exposed capitalist practices to sharp criticism. "That development which capitalism marks over slavery and feudalism consists as much in the methods by means of which labor is coerced as in the mode of production. Capitalism is but the gentleman's method of slavery,"[1] he wrote. Developing this thought on the exploitative nature of capitalism he said, "the evil of capitalism consists in its alienation of the fruit of labor from those who with the toil of their body and the sweat of their brow produce this fruit."[2] Nkrumah displayed an understanding of the essence of the "newest" theories on capitalism, theories designed to mask its predatory nature. In criticizing these apologetic theories, which were based on the relative rise in the living standards of working men and women that had taken place, he wrote, "the proportion of distribution of value between exploited and exploiter is kept constant" and "any increase in levels of production must mean a greater quantity, but not in proportion, of value accruing to the exploited."[3]

Socialism's mission, Nkrumah thought, was to ensure that the state of colonialism was quickly left behind, that post-colonial society was modernized and that the people's urgent needs were satisfied. However, the Ghanian President's rejection of capitalism did not signify his adoption of scientific socialism. This he considered unacceptable for Africa in its "pure form" and he argued that it had to be adapted to specifically African conditions. Once Ghana had gained its independence, Kwame Nkrumah set to work on his own theory of "African socialism."

Nkrumah was not alone in trying to create a new "original" theory. After the African countries gained their independence a large number of "national-type socialisms" made their appearance. Independence had only just been gained. African ideologists were filled with a desire to show the world that Africa was unique, that it was capable not just of copying the achievements of the rest of the world but of working out its own concept of social development which would be profoundly African in essence. This delusion, widespread in Africa for some years, was the cause of serious miscalculations in both the domestic and foreign policies of many African countries. In this connection it is appropriate to

---

[1]*Consciencism: . . .*, p. 72.
[2]Ibid., p. 76.
[3]Ibid., p. 79.

recall what Lenin said about revolutionary theory: "That theory cannot be thought up. It *grows out* of the sum total of the revolutionary experience and the revolutionary thinking of all countries in the world."[1]

No one succeeded in creating a "pure" ideology. Some African leaders used reformist "democratic socialist" ideas extensively to cloak their policy of cooperating with imperialism. Others, including Kwame Nkrumah, tried to combine a few Marxist tenets as well as various theories from petty bourgeois socialism with traditional African views on man and society.

The most complete and systematic description of Nkrumah's conception of socialism is presented in his 1964 book, *Consciencism: Philosophy and Ideology for Decolonization and Development with Particular Reference to the African Revolution.* Consciencism, according to Nkrumah, would "give the theoretical basis for an ideology whose aim shall be to contain the African experience of Islamic and Euro-Christian presence as well as the experience of the traditional African society, and, by gestation, employ them for the harmonious development of that society."[2] In other words, an all-embracing ideology that could unify African society and become the guiding force behind social progress would replace the various traditional and extrinsic, frequently conflicting ideologies of the past. The socialist orientation of this ideology, Nkrumah believed, was ensured by the egalitarian principles on which traditional African society was founded.

Many revolutionary democrats have taken the distinctive features of patriarchal African society into account in their work. The African community, a stable socio-economic structure, sets African society apart. As revolutionary democrats see it, they must bring the community "up to date" and give it new functions in keeping with the tasks building a non-capitalist society involves. As is well known Engels assigned the community a similar role. But in this instance a scientific analysis of the traditional community, its positive and negative aspects is essential. Admiration of the past and an uncritical attitude toward it leads to a theoretical reconstruction of traditionalism and to incorrect conclusions concerning the African states' current stage of social development.

Idealizing patriarchal African society, Nkrumah wrote, "The traditional

---

[1] V. I. Lenin, "The Voice of an Honest French Socialist", *Collected Works,* Vol. 21, Progress Publishers, Moscow, 1977, p. 354.

[2] *Consciencism . . . ,* p. 70.

face of Africa includes an attitude towards man which can only be described, in its social manifestation, as being socialist. This arises from the fact that man is regarded in Africa as primarily a spiritual being, a being endowed originally with a certain inward dignity, integrity and value."[1] Nkrumah called interpersonal relations in African society "communalistic," i.e. everyone is equal and each has a responsibility towards all. Therefore, he concludes that traditional society is classless and, furthermore, that "Marxist type" classes could not arise in such a society. "If one seeks the social-political ancestor of socialism, one must go to communalism,"[2] Nkrumah wrote.

Nkrumah's analysis of African society ignored the fact that the various regions of Africa developed in quite different ways and that prior to the arrival of the colonialists, feudal relations and, hence, social stratification had existed in some regions of the continent. True, this stratification was not of a clearly defined nature and for this reason class conflict was not sharp. Kwame Nkrumah acknowledged that colonialism had caused certain changes in traditional African society but he saw its influence only in the introduction of new values, some of which eroded the traditional way of life, while others merged with it.

Thus, Nkrumah denied not only the presence of classes in traditional African society but also the inevitability of their rise in modern Africa. This thesis was the basis of Nkrumah's "African socialism," which he thought would come into being as social reforms were carried out and the undesirable changes that had occurred under colonialism were eradicated. He wrote, "from the ancestral line of communalism, the passage to socialism lies in reform, because the underlying principles are the same."[3] Here Nkrumah clearly reveals that he does not adequately understand the nature or principles of socialism as a social system. Instead he reduces them to humanistic and ethical tenets. As far as smoothing over conflicts of class interests is concerned, this approach has proved to be invalid not just in Ghana but in Africa as a whole. By the time *Consciencism* ... was published there were already definite signs of an intensification of the class struggle on the continent brought on by the deepening of the African revolution's social aspects. Sensing the vulnerability of his fundamental tenets, Kwame Nkrumah felt it necessary to

[1] Ibid., p. 68.
[2] Ibid., p. 73.
[3] Ibid., p. 74.

make the proviso that "in its political aspect philosophical consciencism is faced with realities of colonialism, imperialism, disunity and lack of development. Singly and collectively these four mitigate against the realization of a social justice based on ideas of true equality."[1]

Not acknowledging the class struggle, on the one hand, or the clear growth of contradictions in African society, on the other, Nkrumah began to construct abstract models in which he attempted to take in the whole range of complex processes occurring in the African revolution. These models were primarily composed of what Nkrumah termed positive and negative action. He defined positive action as "the sum of those forces seeking social justice in terms of the destruction of oligarchic exploitation and oppression. Negative action will correspondingly represent the sum of those forces tending to prolong colonial subjugation and exploitation."[2] Thus, Kwame Nkrumah defined African society not by its class structure but by the political views of its members. Such general evaluations of the interaction between social forces would have reflected the political situation to a certain degree if they had supplemented a class analysis. But Nkrumah never applied the term "class" to African reality. He used it only to characterize capitalist and socialist society while the class struggle was for him something that existed with reference to relations between the African countries and imperialism, but not within African society itself.

Nkrumah believed that positive action had to be "armed with an ideology which ... shall equip it with a regenerative concept of the world and life ... "[3] if it was to combat colonialism. Consciencism was to be that ideology. In order to make it more scientific Nkrumah set to work developing the philosophical foundations of this teaching.

Materialism was said to be the theoretical basis of consciencism. The idea that matter exists absolutely and independently and is infinite runs through all of Kwame Nkrumah's philosophical discourses. However, upon closer analysis it becomes clear that Nkrumah's materialism is of a spontaneous rather than a scientific nature. While he recognizes the objective existence of the external world, on the question of the relationship between material and spiritual substance he takes a dualistic position. When considering this, the fundamental question of philosophy, Nkrumah speaks

[1] *Consciencism ... , p. 98.
[2] Ibid., p. 99.
[3] Ibid., p. 105.

of how philosophical consciencism differs from a) "extreme materialism" (meaning Marxism), which postulates the sole reality of matter, and b) idealism, which recognises the primacy of the spiritual. He declared that his philosophy removed this "philosophical perplexity" and that "the interaction of mind and body is accepted as a fact."[1] Having identified Marxism with vulgar materialism, Nkrumah did not grasp the scientific approach to the relationship between the material and the spiritual, an approach which never placed those two categories in opposition but considered them in terms of their interrelationship. Kwame Nkrumah's conception of how matter and spirit relate was not consistently scientific either. He placed the mind on the same level as matter even though material substance is given priority. "Philosophical consciencism does not assert the sole reality of matter. Rather it asserts the primary reality of matter,"[2] wrote Nkrumah. For him the mind, having originated in matter, acquires absolute autonomy. As has long been known, attempts to go beyond the boundaries of philosophy's fundamental question lead to idealism.

The belief some African politicians have in the autonomy of the mind and its independence with regard to matter can be explained by the role the subjective factor plays in Africa. As a result of the general economic, social and cultural underdevelopment of African countries, enormous significance in the transformation of society has been given to the subjective factor, the superstructure. At times it seems to some revolutionary democrats that it is the subjective (the revolutionary will, the revolutionary mind) which has the decisive role to play in history, that the subjective is fundamental to changes in the objective.

In this connection we must consider the relationship between the base and the superstructure, between theory and practice. Scientific socialism recognizes the active role the superstructure plays in the historical process, and the influence it has on all aspects of the basis. However, the base always plays the decisive role. As for the relationship between theory and practice, Marxism-Leninism extracts theory from practice. This is not the case with Nkrumah, who maintained that emergent ideology "seeks to affect social milieu." "The ideology of a society," he wrote, "is total. It embraces the whole life of a people ... "[3] In other words, practice is subordinate to theory. As a result of the absolutization

[1]Ibid., pp. 86–87.
[2]Ibid., p. 88.
[3]Ibid., pp. 56, 59.

of the role theory plays in social processes and the disregard shown for objective conditions, consciencism was proclaimed to be a universal theory applicable not just to Africa but to "all dependent countries or emerging nations."[1]

Kwame Nkrumah frequently stated that philosophical consciencism is a dialectical teaching. In fact, however, consciencism limits its dialecticism mostly to a recognition of the main category employed by materialist dialectics – contradictions. Other categories and principles, such as "the transition from quantitative to qualitative changes" and "the negation of the negation", are ignored.

Consciencism, Nkrumah wrote, "conceives matter as a plenum of tensions giving rise to dialectical change ... and since tension implies incipient change, matter must have the power of self-motion ... Without self-motion dialectical change would be impossible."[2] This is an important feature of Kwame Nkrumah's philosophy. Here he reveals the motive force behind and source of all development. He regards the movement of matter as spontaneous, not as a result of the action of external forces. Hence, consciencism is, in essence, atheistic. It repudiates the idea of supernatural intervention. Although Nkrumah declared that "philosophical consciencism, even though deeply rooted in materialism, is not necessarily atheistic,"[3] he appears to have done this out of tactical considerations, out of a desire to make his ideology an ideology "for all." Nkrumah's attitude towards religion was fairly contradictory. His declaration that he considered himself a non-denominational Christian and, at the same time, a "social Marxist" is well known. On the other hand, he once called religion "an instrument of bourgeois social reaction"[4] and cautioned African revolutionaries against using it to attain political ends, calling such action opportunistic. "Seizing the slightest of these chances," he wrote, "they in fact take two steps backward for the one step forward in order to enjoy a transitory consolidation based on a common religious belief and practice." This tactic "can only create more problems than it promises to solve. For certain, it will check the advancing social consciousness of the people."[5] However, Nkrumah called for a cautious and

---

[1] *Some Essential Features of Nkrumahism,* The Spark Publications, Accra, 1964, p. 44.

[2] *Consciencism ...* , pp. 93, 90.

[3] *Consciencism ...* , p. 84.

[4] Ibid., p. 13

[5] ιDιι

flexible approach to religious belief. Citing Marx, he said that religion was also "a social fact, and must be understood before it can be tackled."[1] This formulation of the question raises Nkrumah above both those revolutionary democrats who try to use religion to achieve narrow pragmatic goals and those who fight for its immediate eradication from the consciousness of the African masses. In any society, and particularly in African society where a certain inertness and conservatism continue to characterize the mass consciousness, the atheistic education of the masses requires sustained, laborious work which can be successful only if it involves the dissemination of the natural scientific views of the Marxist world outlook. The Nkrumahist approach to social contradictions differs radically from the Marxist-Leninist approach. Kwame Nkrumah examined social contradictions and their bearers not by means of a concrete socio-class analysis but rather by introducing the abstract categories "positive action" and "negative action" mentioned above. This approach does not permit an analysis of the actual distribution of forces or of the contradictions between them, for in place of the complex picture of class contradictions it depicts a society split into "the forces of progress" and "the forces of reaction."

Kwame Nkrumah automatically applied philosophy's fundamental question to society. Thus, for example, he wrote: "By reason of the connection of idealism with an oligarchy and of materialism with an egalitarianism, the opposition of idealism and materialism in the same society is paralleled by the opposition of conservative and progressive forces on the social level."[2] Yes, materialism and the materialist interpretation of history are in the masses' fundamental interests while idealism is in the interests of the exploiters but the mass consciousness of Africans is still characterized by the presence of idealistic thought processes. The development of philosophical problems in Nkrumah's ideology is, to a large extent, of an applied nature and serves as the motivation for political practice and the basis for actions suggested by the political struggle and life itself.

Kwame Nkrumah devoted a great deal of his attention to developing ethical principles for an African society that had chosen socialism as its goal. He used the concept of "the African personality" as the basis of his

[1]Ibid.
[2]Ibid., p. 75.

theoretical substantiation of "African socialism's" moral ideas. African ideologists armed themselves with this concept in order to "rehabilitate the Black man" so that he might take his rightful place in the history of mankind. Arising first in the area of culture (Aimé Césaire, Leopold Senghor) and later taken up by other ideologists who expanded it, this concept has never been clearly defined by any of them. Every version is, however, based on the supposed traditional humanism of African society. "The African personality," Nkrumah wrote, "is itself defined by the cluster of humanist principles which underlie the traditional African society."[1] Thus, Nkrumah resolves the fundamental problem of ethics – the question of the source and basis of moral ideas – not by taking a materialist approach; he deduces the "African personality's" moral ideas not from the modes of production which have developed over time, nor from the progress of material and spiritual culture but from an extrahistorical abstraction – the humanistic nature of the African. This formulation of the question places Nkrumah in the same camp with the advocates of ethical relativism which denies that ethics are determined by social milieu.

Nkrumah tried to invest the "African personality" with social content. He saw the moral standard of the African embodied in the man who is dedicated, modest, honest and educated, the man who gives himself completely to the service of his country and humanity, who finds greed repulsive and hates vanity. This man's strength, he said, lay in his modesty, while his greatness lay in his moral purity. Without question this type of citizen is absolutely essential if a new society is to be built, but Nkrumah thought he could be created not through the inculcation of socialist ethics but by returning to traditional moral codes. "The emancipation of the African continent is the emancipation of man," he wrote. "This requires two aims: first, the restitution of the egalitarianism of human society, and, second, the logistic mobilization of all our resources towards the attainment of that restitution."[2] It is important to note that even though Nkrumah constantly turned to the past – indeed it was almost a fetish – he had a fairly clear picture of Africa's future, which he linked to socialism. Nkrumah characterized socialism as a society in which "the study and mastery of nature has a humanist impulse, and is directed not towards a profiteering accomplishment, but the affording of ever increasing satisfaction for the material and spiritual needs of the greatest

[1]Ibid., p. 79.
[2]Ibid., p. 78.

number."[1] "Socialism," he stressed, "assumes the public ownership of the means of production, the land and its resources, and the use of those means in fulfilment of the people's needs."[2]

At the same time socialism to Nkrumah was, to a large extent, not the result of objective socio-economic development but a moral category. Moral relations and ideas concerning moral perfection were key to the way in which Nkrumah conceptualized socialism. This approach to social-ism is not new. Petty bourgeois and social-democratic "ethical socialist" theoreticians who attempted to combine scientific socialism with Kant's ethical principles also set ethics the task of eliminating contradictions from social relations.

An analysis of Nkrumahism reveals that in the area of theory it signified an attempt to combine various tenets of Marxism-Leninism, petty bour-geois socialism and the traditional African world outlook. From Marxism Nkrumahism borrowed a recognition of contradictions, the inevitability of the transition to socialism and the arguments used in the critique of capitalism. Petty bourgeois socialism was the source of the denial of the class struggle, the substitution of the term "the people" for classes and the belief in an evolutionary path towards socialism. Traditionalism was reflected in the conviction that African society was egalitarian by nature, the rejection of "borrowed" ideologies and the belief that Africa was destined to take a "special" path.

When Africa ceased to be a continent of colonies, it needed an ideology capable of explaining both its past and its prospects for the future. The only ideology which fully meets these criteria is scientific socialism. But in the early '60s it had not yet become the ideological weapon used by the majority of African revolutionaries. Meanwhile, the objective demands of social development required that the "ideological vacuum" which had formed when independence was gained be filled. Despite the obvious influence of external factors Nkrumahism, like other theories put forward by revolutionary democrats, is in essence a reflection, although not always an adequate one, of real, complex and contradictory processes that occur in any state that has opted for a socialist future.

Even though Marxism did not become Nkrumah's world outlook and he made use of only some of its tenets, the influence scientific socialism had on his ideological views is not in question. Nkrumahism was transitional

[1]Ibid., p. 76.
[2]*Africa Must Unite*, p. 119.

in nature. It could not be a long-lasting ideology not only because it combined incompatible elements but also because, as Lenin said, "the *only* choice is – either bourgeois or socialist ideology. There is no middle course (for mankind has not created a 'third' ideology, and, moreover, in a society torn by class antagonisms there can never be a non-class or an above-class ideology)."[1] The essential aspects of various theories on "national-type socialisms", advanced in the first years of independence by certain revolutionary democrats, had a great deal in common with concepts put forward by conservative African ideologists. With time a differentiation occurred in the theories of "African socialism:" the progressive trends moved closer towards scientific socialism while the reactionary trends clearly revealed their pro-bourgeois essence. Nkrumahism contained the elements necessary to bring about its evolution towards scientific socialism and this did indeed occur during the final phase of Kwame Nkrumah's ideological work.

[1] V. I. Lenin, "What Is to Be Done?", *Collected Works*, Vol. 5, p. 384.

VII. Nkrumahism in Domestic Policy

The domestic policies Kwame Nkrumah pursued were largely determined by his ideological and political views. At the same time, however, adjustments in these policies were brought about by the objective socio-economic and political conditions as life developed in independent Ghana. Many of his theories arose out of the necessity of validating the practical action that circumstances had prompted the government to take. These theories represented an original understanding of reality.

After the country's path of development was determined in the early '60s, Nkrumah's socio-economic policies became distinctly anti-imperialist, anti-capitalist and anti-feudal in nature. They were designed to lay the foundations of Ghanian society's socialist orientation.

The radical change in government policy was most clearly revealed in the role and place the state sector was now assigned in socio-economic development. A state sector had existed in Ghana even prior to 1961. Kwame Nkrumah's government inherited railways, thermal power stations and the port of Takoradi from the colonial administration. In the first years of independence state enterprises were established in the service sphere and companies jointly owned by the state and foreign private interests were set up. Examples of the latter type of company are the Black Star Shipping Line and Ghana Airways. For the most part the state owned those enterprises that could not belong to the weak local private interests due to the volume of capital required. The state's economic functions were limited to the regulation of development and did not include a broad range of production-related tasks. Once the country had opted for the socialist orientation the state sector took on an anti-imperialist and anti-capitalist tenor. Nkrumah came to the conclusion that the size of the state sector and the character of its development depend on the political system which is chosen – capitalism or socialism. Henceforward the determining role in economic development was assigned

105

to the public sector, which was to become the material foundation of development along the non-capitalist path. "State enterprises are the main economic pillars on which we expect to build our socialist State,"[1] the Ghanian President declared.

Kwame Nkrumah's government was the first in Tropical Africa to begin the nationalization process. The merchant fleet, civil aviation, five of the seven British mining enterprises, a Dutch diamond mining company and a major foreign trading company, Leventis, all became state property. The Bank of Ghana and the Investment Bank, which financed the construction and modernization of state sector enterprises, were set up. A state monopoly on foreign trade was established. These measures severely undercut the position of foreign capital in Ghana's economy.

The government's anti-imperialist economic policies were combined with anti-capitalist measures designed to monitor local private enterprise and restrict its activities. New state companies and enterprises were set up to take the place of private interests in industry, finance and commerce. The foreign private interests Nkrumah attracted to help the country's economic development were required to work with the state rather than with domestic private interests so that the private sector and its ties with foreign private interests would not be strengthened.

Nkrumah believed that the socialist-oriented economy should be planned. Furthermore, planning was seen not as a simple expansion of the state's economic functions – the capitalist conception of planning – but as a process by which the state regulates the entire socio-economic complex and steers it toward socialism. Nkrumah wrote, "A new country needs to initiate central nationwide planning fitting the required activities of each region into the overall program."[2]

When a country chooses a particular concept of planning it has, in essence, chosen in which direction it will develop. The first five-year plan independent Ghana set out to fulfill in 1959 reflected the Ghanian leadership's conviction that the country could follow a "third path". The realization that this had been a mistaken belief led to the discontinuation of the plan to all intents and purposes in 1961. That same year a national commission headed by the President was created to work out a new plan. Ghana's choice in favor of socialism was consolidated in the seven-year plan (1963-1969) that commission produced.

[1] *The Ghanaian Times,* January 13, 1965, p. 6.
[2] *Africa Must Unite,* p. 64.

The economy's planned development ran into a number of difficulties, both objective and subjective, which, as experience has shown, are characteristic for all developing countries that have chosen a socialist future. The planning was not comprehensive in nature and primarily affected the state sector. The state did not occupy the commanding heights in the economy. It did not have the economic levers with which it could effectively bring pressure to bear on the private and traditional sectors that played an important role in the economy. Unable to regulate these two sectors, it could only influence them indirectly. The economy of Ghana, like those of other African states, was multistructural in nature and the economic policies of the Nkrumah government were based on a recognition of the necessity of having a mixed economy. As Nkrumah saw it, the economy had five sectors: "1) State enterprises; 2) enterprises owned by foreign private interests; 3) enterprises jointly owned by State and foreign private interests; 4) cooperatives, and 5) small-scale Ghanaian private enterprises."[1] The Work and Happiness program adopted by the CPP in 1962 reflected, on the political level, the changes that had occurred in the socio-economic sphere, set the task of developing the state and cooperative sectors at an accelerated rate. These would gradually supplant all other structures and eventually play the dominant role in the economy.

Industrialization

Nkrumah believed that it would be easier to change the colonial economic structure if plan-based industrialization were expanded. The ultimate objective was to develop a technologically modern, diversified economic structure capable of guaranteeing high growth rates for the economy as a whole as well as the achievement of economic and social progress. "Socialism . . . will continue to remain a slogan until industrialization is achieved,"[2] he said.

Ghana scored significant successes in establishing new industries. Enterprises appeared which utilized local raw materials and turned out essential goods that the country had been obliged to import before. Now the republic produced matches, shoes, sweets, chocolate, canned fruit and vegetables, beverages, chemicals, nails, automobile tires, cement and

[1]Ibid., p. 121.
[2]*Revolutionary Path,* p. 190.

much, much more. The resulting reduction in the volume of imports strengthened the country's economy. All of the new industrial facilities supplemented the state sector. But the biggest investments were made in large-scale projects that were expected to bring about significant changes in the economic structure. The largest deep-water port in West Africa, Tema Port, was built. There, in place of the old fishing village, a major industrial complex with aluminium, steel, oil refining, textile and food processing components rose. In Tarkwa construction was begun on a gold refining plant which made it possible for Ghana to sell gold ingots on the world market. Tractor and motorcar assembly plants along with many other industrial enterprises were included in the seven-year plan.

Kwame Nkrumah had a special interest in the Volta River Project. Back in 1952 he had proposed that a dam and hydroelectric power station with a capacity of over 800,000 kw be built in Akosombo on the Volta River. This project would bring water to the drought-stricken savanna and provide the country with cheap electricity. The existing thermal power stations operated on expensive imported fuel – coal and oil. Neither the British government nor British financiers would agree to provide the funding for this major project. Once independence had been gained, Nkrumah turned his attention to the Volta River Project once again. Specialists estimated the cost at 70 million pounds sterling. The state was able to provide only half of that sum. In 1958, during a visit to the U.S. Nkrumah received a promise from President Eisenhower that the U.S. would provide the necessary loans. Preparations got underway in Akosombo. But then a series of events occurred which clearly revealed the equivocal nature of imperialist "aid." After Nkrumah criticized U.S. foreign policy in addresses to the fifteenth session of the U.N. General Assembly and the Belgrade Conference of Non-Aligned Countries, the signing of the economic aid agreement – scheduled for October 5, 1961 – was called off by the Americans. The ruling circles in the United States wished to be assured of the Ghanian government's "moderate" political orientation. Nkrumah stood firm. He sent a letter asking President Eisenhower to inform him whether the U.S. government was planning to keep its promise. The news that the Soviet Union had shouldered the responsibility for financing the construction of a dam and hydroelectric power station on the Volta made the Americans, who did not want a repeat of "the Aswan Dam situation", more tractable. In early 1962 an agreement was signed under which the U.S., Britain and the World Bank agreed to provide Ghana with loans worth 35 million pounds sterling. By early 1966 the Volta River Project had been completed.

The Nkrumah government refused to limit itself to economic ties with the capitalist countries. Great assistance to Ghana's economic development was provided by the socialist countries and the Soviet Union, first and foremost. On February 2, 1962 in Accra representatives of Ghana and the USSR signed an agreement on a massive loan to be repaid on easy terms over a period of many years, and a technical and economic cooperation pact. In general outline they had been agreed upon during Nkrumah's visit to the USSR and the subsequent visit to Moscow by a Ghanian trade delegation. The Soviet Union helped build a great many works, supplied the necessary machinery and equipment for them and assisted in training national cadres.

Implementation of the industrialization policy brought about important social changes. Industrialization played a decisive role not just in overcoming economic backwardness and decreasing the country's dependence on imperialism but, to a certain extent, in transforming social relations as well. One important consequence of the industrialization policy was the growth of the working class's numerical strength and degree of vocational skill. An increase was seen in the number of workers employed in modern branches of the economy, particularly in manufacturing and construction.

However, the rise in the construction of major industrial works, projects requiring enormous capital investments by Ghanian standards with a financial return only in the distant future, also had a number of negative features. Many projects were not solidly based economically. Frequently they were the result of a voluntaristic approach to development problems. "Our aim, under this [seven-year] Plan, is to build in Ghana a socialist State which accepts full responsibility for promoting the well-being of the masses."[1] In the lifetime of a single generation Nkrumah intended to create a developed industrial society in a country which did not possess sufficient resources for this – economic, financial or otherwise. Ghana remained an agrarian society with a one-crop agricultural system. The implementation of an advanced economic policy when the way had not been paved by the course of social evolution, when a certain minimum of prerequisites did not exist and when the state did not occupy the commanding heights in the economy led to significant complications in the country's economic situation. Heavy industry was built up at the expense of other branches of the economy, particularly agriculture, which remained the basis of the country's economy.

[1]*Revolutionary Path,* p. 190.

Given the absence of extensive domestic accumulations, economic development plans in Ghana, as in other developing countries, were dependent on foreign capital. But, as experience has shown, foreign private interests are reluctant to become partners in the implementation of socialist oriented socio-economic policies notwithstanding the privileges they are granted for doing so. In Ghana the Capital Investment Act was passed in 1963. It provided foreign investors with broad opportunities and guarantees. Kwame Nkrumah said, "We welcome foreign investors in a spirit of partnership. They can earn their profits here provided they leave us an agreed portion for promoting the welfare and happiness of our people . . . "[1] The seven-year plan stipulated that around half of the state capital investments in economic development would be funded by foreign loans and subsidies. Foreign capitalists, however, were not in any hurry to invest in Ghana: they hoped that the radical regime would soon crumble. In 1965 the influx of investments from abroad was a mere tenth of the sum envisioned by the seven-year plan and this caused considerable damage to the country's economy. The example of Ghana demonstrated once again that reliance on extensive involvement by foreign investors in the development of countries with progressive governments is highly problematical and can contribute to economic and political instability.

Kwame Nkrumah's appeals for assistance from the International Monetary Fund and the World Bank met with demands that fundamental changes be made in Ghana's economic policies, including the suspension of new projects, a halt to subsidies to state enterprises, more "liberal" policies towards foreign private investment and, most importantly, revision of the bilateral agreements with the socialist countries, "with a view of reducing their harmful impact on the Ghana economy"[2]. Nkrumah categorically rejected the discriminatory conditions laid down by these organizations, which are controlled by the U.S. financial oligarchy. However, imperialist blackmail did not stop there. By manipulating cacao prices on the world capitalist market, Western monopolies were able to deal a serious blow to the Ghanian economy as the export of cacao beans remained the state's main source of revenue. Between 1954 and 1965 cacao prices were reduced six-fold at the same time as prices on imported goods saw a steady increase. The fact that cacao prices began to rise once

---

[1]Quoted in: Kwesi Armah, *Ghana: Nkrumah's Legacy,* Rex Collings, London, 1974, p. 60.

[2]Quoted in: Björn Beckman, *Organising the Farmers: Cocoa Politics and National Development in Ghana,* The Scandinavian Institute of African Studies, Uppsala, 1978, p. 18.

more after the Nkrumah government was overthrown speaks to the very specific aim the imperialist states had in pursuing this policy.

Ghana's economic difficulties were also aggravated to a large extent by the fact that most state enterprises operated at a loss despite large injections of capital by the state. This situation was not unique to Ghana. State sector enterprises in many developing countries frequently operate at a loss due to the general backwardness of the economy, the lack of skilled national cadres (particularly engineers, technicians and administrators), the narrowness of the domestic market and the incompetitiveness of their products on the world market. In addition, by virtue of their enormous cost many industrial works only begin to turn a net profit after being in operation for many years. As experience has shown, state sector industrial enterprises are usually unprofitable only during the initial stage of industrialization. After that, if well-founded economic policies are pursued these enterprises can and should operate in the black.

Agriculture

In implementing non-capitalist development policies the Nkrumah government gave a great deal of attention to the establishment of cooperatives and state farms as a way of modernizing agriculture. The creation of the cooperative sector was considered an important part of the complex of socio-economic measures the state took to promote social progress. The cooperative movement in Ghana had seen some growth even before independence was gained. For the most part, it was represented by marketing cooperatives which purchased cacao beans from peasants. After independence was declared this type of cooperative society was developed and extended to other branches of agriculture. The most popular type of cooperative society, it played an important role in the economic and social evolution of the Ghanian village with its poorly developed productive forces and patriarchal structure.

However, marketing cooperatives did not solve the problems of restructuring the colonial economy, liquidating the multistructural economic system and reconstructing the village – the goals of the Nkrumah government. That is why particular attention was given to the development of peasant production cooperatives. The most prevalent type was the cooperative farm where the peasants worked in the collective field several days a week but spent the majority of their time working on the individual plots that brought them their main income. These were, to be more precise, the forerunners of the production cooperative, and engendered new types of social relations in agriculture. The creation of youth settlements in the virgin lands represented an attempt to form a more advanced type of cooperative. In these cooperatives, which Nkrumah believed to be the prototype of the future Ghanian village, the means of production were collectively owned and the principle of payment in accordance with work performed was introduced. These settlements were to be supplied with electricity and water and plans called for the centralized construction of housing, community centers, aid posts and schools. By 1965 forty such settlements had been built. The Nkrumah government did all it could to help the cooperators, providing them with loans, farm machinery and seed.

Along with encouraging agriculturalists to form cooperatives the Ghanian government pursued the policy of creating a state agricultural sector. It was hoped that this sector would ensure the existence of a domestic food base and accelerate the growth of agricultural production. First, the state established control over the purchase of farm goods from producers and a monopoly on their export, entrusting this job to state companies. Then the Nkrumah government began to set up state farms. The first such farms were established in 1962 at experimental stations which had formerly belonged to the colonial administration. In 1966 there were 114 state farms in Ghana. Plans called for them to become the main source of industrial raw materials and a few types of food. Ghana was given considerable assistance in setting up state farms by the socialist countries. The Soviet Union supplied machinery, tools, construction materials, fertilizers and chemicals. The technical and administrative personnel of Ghana's state farms received instruction from Soviet specialists in Ghana and the USSR.

These broad agrarian reforms encountered a number of difficulties of both an objective and subjective nature. The main obstacle to the reconstruction of the Ghanian village was its backwardness. Government efforts had little effect due to tribal, religious and hierarchical survivals as well as the low level of education which prevailed in the village. The strengthening of the cooperatives' and state farms' production base was also hindered by their low initial technical and economic level and by the state's lack of resources. The final factor is particularly important as agriculture in Africa is not a source of funds for the development of industry but must itself be subsidized. In Ghana the cooperative and state sectors did not make a significant contribution to total agricultural production. More than 98 per-cent was produced by the private sector which featured a rural bourgeois stratum – well-to-do farmers who utilized hired labor.

The rise in the number of production coperatives led to attempts to "urge on" the process of cooperation, to disregard the principle of voluntariness, the dissipation of state resources and the misuse of what little farm machinery there was. In the majority of cooperatives the wage system was of a levelling nature which was not inducive to the growth of productivity. State farms operated at a loss for the most part and were subsidized by the state. Beyond these objective difficulties the development of this progressive form of agricultural production was also slowed by the practice of hiring extra hands – motivated by the desire to reduce unemployment – as well as by the absence of skilled cadres. Great harm was also done by corruption in the administrative apparatus.

In general, Kwame Nkrumah's agricultural policies were aimed at eliminating communal production relations, at preventing the development of capitalism in the countryside and at creating the prerequisites for an agricultural system based on socialist principles. This was begun by organizing small farmers into production cooperatives where they had access to farm machinery and could learn modern farming methods. The establishment of state farms furthered the liquidation of the multistructural economy, the steady expansion of state ownership of the means of production and the mobilization of those citizens who had not been drawn into the economic life of the country earlier to help bring about non-capitalist development. In Ghana paths of agricultural development new to Africa were mapped out and embarked upon, and credit for this goes to the Nkrumah government. The Ghanian experiment in creating state and cooperative sectors in agriculture, a branch of the economy then employing two-thirds of the country's population, is of importance for those African states pursuing socialist oriented policies.

In Ghana, as in other Tropical African countries where the food problem is now exceptionally severe, that which was learned in the course of the Nkrumah government's agricultural experiments has not been consigned to oblivion. Young Ghanaians and a significant portion of the country's intelligentsia are demanding that Ghana take the best from the agricultural achievements "under Nkrumah" and go one step further; nationalize the country's farm land and implement a broad, long-term program for modernizing agricultural production on a progressive basis.

Social welfare

The government of Ghana placed a great deal of emphasis on improving the welfare of the people, particularly of the workers and peasants, and bettering their living conditions. "We shall measure our progress," Nkrumah declared, "by the improvement in the health of our people; by the number of children in school, and by the quality of their education; by the availability of water and electricity in our towns and villages... The welfare of our people is our chief pride, and it is by this that my government will be judged."[1] An eight-hour workday, 45-hour work-week and a guaranteed minimum wage were all established by government decree. In addition a law was passed under which hired labor was provided with social insurance. According to the 1960 census, 66 percent of the country's workers could neither read nor write while the peasantry was almost totally illiterate. In order to bring about profound changes in society the country had to have skilled cadres and to raise the overall level of culture and literacy. In this area Ghana had considerable success. Compulsory free primary education was introduced and the network of schools, colleges and universities was significantly expanded. In the years that independent Ghana was governed by the Nkrumah government, the number of schools more than doubled at every level while enrolments rose three-fold. Great attention was given to the job of training teachers and enrolments in teacher training colleges increased by several hundred percent. The government encouraged the expansion of higher education. New institutions of higher learning rose beside old ones. University College at Legon, formerly a branch of the University of London and a focal point of anti-government forces, became an independent university (Ghana University) and the reactionary European teachers were sacked. The former Kumasi College of Technology became the University of Science and Technology. A new university college was opened in Cape Coast. The country's actual needs were taken into consideration when curricula for schools and institutions of higher learning were drawn up. Their objective was to cultivate practical skills which would be of use in the building of a new life. Kwame Nkrumah did not want to transform Ghana into just a country with a high literacy rate: he wanted to see it contribute to the most advanced branches of learning. At his request the Soviet Union designed and built a reactor for nuclear research and trained Ghanaians to staff it.

[1] I Speak of Freedom, p. 117.

Great success was also scored in the area of health care. Ghana achieved reductions in infant mortality and epidemic diseases, particularly malaria. The objectives of the country's health care programs included expanding the network of free surgeries in rural areas, organizing health services, training midwives, eliminating polluted springs and supplying the population with clean water, constructing sewer systems in cities and eradicating slums. New hospitals were built and old hospitals reconstructed. Doctors began to be trained on a broad scale both in Ghana and abroad. Government programs envisaged a high level of medical care with one doctor for every 10,000 patients.

In effecting its social policies the Ghanian leadership wished, first of all, to improve the economic position of working men and women and to show them and all the world the superiority of independent, progressive development. Despite these subjective aspirations, however, the standard of living remained low. Ghana came up against a problem encountered by many developing countries that aspire to economic independence but do not have significant domestic accumulations. Briefly: how can the accelerated development of industry, which requires enormous material resources, be combined with a steady improvement in the people's standard of living? The majority of African countries face this problem today.

Enormous investments were required to finance industrial works in Ghana. Given the poverty of state accumulations, the steady drop in world prices of cacao (the main source of export revenues), and the policy of restraining the private sector's initiative, the Nkrumah government had to resort to borrowing money from domestic and foreign sources. Most of the loans granted by imperialist countries were short- and medium-term. This was a difficult time for the Ghanian economy. Constant domestic borrowing, increasingly higher taxes and rising prices on consumer goods, the result of a rise in import duties, led to a worsening of the working people's financial position and caused discontent. Due to the catastrophic drop in cacao prices on the world market the Nkrumah government was forced in 1965 significantly to reduce the fixed purchase prices on cacao it had established some time earlier. This dealt a severe blow to all who were engaged in the production of this product, 35 percent of Ghana's peasantry. This measure, together with the mistakes that were made in organizing cooperative agriculture, injured the economic position of a large portion of the country's rural population.

All of these government acts, which were difficult for working men and women to understand, all of the "sacrifices" demanded of the people in the name of the efforts the state was making in the area of economic development, did not boost the government's popularity. The economic development that occurred did not bring in its wake the expected noticeable rise in the people's standard of living as the government had promised. The resulting disillusionment together with the indifference of the masses played into the hands of those forces which strove, with imperialism's support, to turn Ghana from its chosen path.

Kwame Nkrumah's socio-economic policies objectively furthered the creation of the prerequisites necessary for the socialist transformation of Ghanian society. However, the Ghanian leader's desire to "speed up" the introduction of socialist-type social relations led to a number of errors in what were, on the whole, sound policies. These mistakes harmed the national economy and narrowed the social basis on which the implementation of any progressive reforms could rest.

Today, when sufficiently rich experience in non-capitalist development has been accumulated, it is not hard to see that some of the economic measures the Nkrumah government took were mistakes. But it should not be forgotten that at the start of the '60s Africa had no experience in this area. Ghana was one of the first countries on that continent to set itself the goal of developing socialism. While the goal – the creation of a society "in which each will give according to his ability and receive according to his needs"[1] – was essentially clear to Nkrumah, the means of achieving it had to be determined as solutions were found to urgent practical problems. Kwame Nkrumah relied on assistance from the socialist states, particularly the Soviet Union.

The West saw this as a threat, and imperialist circles went to no small ends to discredit the Nkrumah government and damage the country's economy. This ultimately helped pave the way for the reactionary coup d'état.

Along with these socio-economic tasks the Ghanian leadership had the important task of creating a new type of state. It was on the state that the task of eliminating colonialism in the economic, political and spiritual spheres of the country's life was placed immediately after independence was declared. Lenin wrote: "The key question of every revolution is undoubtedly the question of state power. Which class holds power

[1] *I Speak of Freedom*, p. 165.

decides everything."[1] In Ghana, as in the other countries of Tropical Africa, the main classes – the bourgeoisie and the proletariat – were relatively small and weak. In this situation intermediate social forces exerted power, and state power was not of a clearly defined class nature. However, this does not mean that the state did not have its own distinct social aspect. Which classes have their interests represented by state power determines the state's social nature. In Ghana, which had been developing along the non-capitalist path since the start of the '60s, the most politically active section of the intermediate strata – the revolutionary democrats – was in power. Their policy of fostering profound social change was in the long-term interests of the working masses.

The CPP's Work and Happiness program adopted in 1962, declared the government of Ghana to be the government of the workers, farmers and peasants. It went on to proclaim that the government pursued a policy of socialist reconstruction in the interests of the working people. This definition of the social nature of the state on the path of progressive reforms reflected to a certain extent the disposition of social forces at the stage of non-capitalist development and represented an important step forward, away from Nkrumah's recent convictions concerning the supra-class nature of power, away from the desire to create a "welfare state." CPP program documents and the essence of the socio-economic and political measures the government took show that, after the choice had been made in favor of socialism the state was, in terms of its objectives, a tool by which the working people exercised their dominion over the bourgeoisie. It is another matter that these objectives were not always consistently realized due to a number of objective difficulties, and that the leadership did not take a clear-cut position on a number of questions relating to domestic political development.

State apparatus

Ghana was the first country in Tropical Africa to deal with the problem of eliminating the colonial political system and creating a national state apparatus. The young independent state inherited a political infrastructure from the British which had been put together during the colonial period. The situation was further complicated by the fact that the 1957

[1] V. I. Lenin, "One of the Fundamental Questions of the Revolution", *Collected Works,* Vol. 25, p. 370.

Constitution, fashioned by Britain, consolidated the existing political institutions and placed Ghana in a position of dependence. The bourgeois parliament and legal system were retained; the army and foreign trade were under British control. For tactical reasons, Ghana was obliged to adopt this constitution, which preserved in general outline the colonial machinery of state. At the same time, in the first years of independence Ghanian leaders themselves thought that the political system they had inherited could be used to meet the aims of independent development if it was "Africanized." Nkrumah believed that it could be placed at the service of the progressive government simply by replacing British officials with Ghanaians.

By 1964 the state apparatus had been almost completely Africanized. The new revolutionary cadres were insufficient and time was needed to supplement them. That is why officials trained by the British for service in the colonial apparatus still predominated. Without a doubt they were the most competent people available as far as administering the state was concerned, and some of them served the national government loyally and conscientiously. But the majority were too conservative to understand or implement Nkrumah's policies. There were open opponents of the socialist orientation in the civil service, too, and they used their position to discredit it. Educated in the British bourgeois tradition, most Ghanaian civil servants had no conception of the people's practical needs and took a disdainful and superior attitude towards the common people in whose interests they were supposed to implement policy. Kwame Nkrumah's conviction that the bourgeois principle of "political neutrality" should be applied in regard to civil servants helped create an atmosphere of exclusiveness and cliquishness in the state apparatus. In May 1960 the government published a new Charter for the Civil Service which said, in part, that "the principle of loyalty to the State and to the Government ... does not imply participation in party politics. Perhaps the most important feature of the Civil Service is its non-political character."[1]

The majority of civil servants took advantage of the opportunities for personal enrichment their positions opened up to them, and this led to the rise of a bureaucratic bourgeoisie in the country. As private enterprise was restricted, they used the money they accumulated through misappropriation and bribe-taking to buy real estate and luxuries. Thus, Martin Appiah-Danquah, General Secretary of the United Ghana Farmers' Cooperative Council, later admitted to owning four houses, three cars

[1]D. Austin, *Politics in Ghana,* 1946-1960, p. 366.

and seven farms.[1] Government Minister Krobo Edusei built himself a real palace with a fountain, garden, swimming pool and tennis courts. At his housewarming party, the guests ooh'd and ah'd over the hall of mirrors and the antique furniture and chandeliers. But the biggest surprise was in the bedroom. It was a gold bed which Madame Edusei had purchased at a "reasonable" price in London. Against the backdrop of constant calls by the government for economy and self-sacrifice in the interests of socialist reconstruction, this sort of behavior on the part of state officials did a great deal of damage to the idea of socialism. Moreover, the scale of misappropriation and the extravagant lifestyle of the bureaucracy directly injured the economy of Ghana with its modest financial resources.

It would be wrong to say that Kwame Nkrumah did not see the dangers that this corrupt and generally antagonistic state apparatus posed. In 1964 a Ghana Radio commentary stated that the "reaction-ridden administrative machinery" was one of the main forces behind the counterrevolution.[2] However, the Ghanaian leader did not consider it necessary to alter the structure of the state apparatus or its social nature. He preferred to "reshuffle" his government instead. In 1961 Nkrumah spoke out against the "old guard" which had begun the struggle for independence with him and was now wallowing in corruption. Six leading members of the government, including Komla Agbeli Gbedemah, Kojo Botsio, Nathaniel A. Welbeck and Krobo Edusei, were forced to tender their resignations and were named the "growing middle class." However, most of the officials who were appointed in their stead continued to follow the old patterns. Moreover, two members of the "new guard" – Hugh H. Cofie-Crabbe and Tawiah Adamafio – were accused of attempting to assassinate the President in 1962. True, Adamafio, who had once held the post of CPP General Secretary as well as many ministerial posts, denied any involvement in the affair. In his book *By Nkrumah's Side — The Labour and Wounds,* published in 1982, he blames his arrest on the intrigues of enemies of the party. In the wake of these events Nkrumah brought Botsio and Welbeck back into the government. Deepening social contradictions within the country and growing activity on the part of counterrevolutionary forces obliged Nkrumah to look to the party's radical activists for support. In 1965 they were given a number of ministerial posts. They did not, however, significantly influence the decisions that

[1] *The Ghanaian Times,* November 15, 1966, p. 1.
[2] See *West Africa,* January 11, 1964, p. 47.

were subsequently taken. More and more state jobs, particularly in the departments responsible for the President's personal safety, went to members of Nkrumah's tribe, the Nzima. These frequent alterations at the top of the state apparatus did not change the situation for the better. Rather, they reflect the confusion Nkrumah felt as he lost control over events in the country.

The Army

Kwame Nkrumah's policies vis-à-vis the army had a great deal in common with his approach to creating a state apparatus, the only difference being that the Africanization of the army did not begin until 1961. Independent Ghana inherited armed forces created by the British colonial power for one major purpose – to suppress the national liberation movement. Their numerical strength was increased and prestigious arms of the service – a navy and air force – were formed. However, steps were not taken to effect a qualitative reorganization of the national army. Moreover, during the first four years of independence, it remained under the direct command of British officers; the Commander-in-chief of Ghana's armed forces and later the Chief of Staff until September 1961 was the British Major-General Alexander, a man who made no attempt to hide his ultra-conservative views. Antagonistic towards the measures the government took, the British officer corps instilled a spirit of cliquishness and apoliticism in the Ghanian army. Kwame Nkrumah's decision to use foreign officers can be explained by two factors – the absence of Ghanaian officers and his conviction that as long as the armed forces were under "neutral" British command they would not pose a threat to the government.

The training of Ghanaian army officers occurred either under the supervision of British instructors in Ghana or at military colleges in Great Britain. The character of the ideas instilled in the Africans was clearly reflected in the statements made by one of the leaders of the reactionary coup, Major Akwesi A. Afrifa, who emphasized that the military academy in Sandhurst was a school of politics, first and foremost. When these officers replaced the British in 1961, the national army remained in the hands of ultra conservatives who took a hostile attitude toward the Nkrumah government's policies. The army became the main and most dangerous focal point of opposition to the government.

Political and educational work was intentionally not conducted within the armed forces. The Convention People's Party, which attempted to make its influence felt throughout the country, did not have organizations in military units. For the intellectual Nkrumah, the army was "terra incognita" and his position with regard to the armed forces was based on the British idea that the army should not get involved in politics. Even when the army's counterrevolutionary and pro-imperialist learnings became clear to everyone, Nkrumah could not bring himself to initiate a radical restructuring of it. Instead, he began to set up military units subordinated to him personally, a fact that caused widespread displeasure among officers, including those who were loyal to the government. Equally unpopular with the military was the government's decision to set up a national militia drawn from the civilian population whose job it would be to defend state institutions at times of crisis. Conservative officers regarded these actions as an attempt on Nkrumah's part to encroach upon their privileged position. The decisive clash between military and civilian authorities was only a matter of time.

The CPP

Kwame Nkrumah assigned the main role in the progressive reconstruction of society to his party. "I am convinced," ne declared, "that the Convention People's Party, based as it is on the support of the overwhelming majority of the people, is best able to carry through our economic plans and build a socialist state."[1] The Convention People's Party established itself as a revolutionary-democratic party in the early '60s when, after a period of searching for a reformist "third path," its leaders made a firm choice in favor of socialism. Ghana's political development during the transitional period was distinguished by the fact that the struggle to determine a socio-economic orientation was conducted not just within the governing party but with the opposition, legal until 1964, in the form of the United Party, a political coalition of all the reactionary forces. To a large extent this struggle on two fronts promoted the consolidation and radicalization of the anti-imperialist and anti-capitalist forces within the CPP. Nevertheless, the CPP continued to be an association of heterogeneous social forces that had come together, for the most part, in the years of the anti-colonial struggle. It could boast a glorious past. At the current stage of the revolution, however, its organizational structure was not appropriate to the new conditions, although Nkrumah maintained that

[1]*Africa Must Unite,* pp. 128-129.

Ghanian experience, internal conditions and the situation in the world around them had been taken into account when it was forged.

The President of Ghana believed that since the bulk of the country's population had an interest in building socialism, socialist reforms should be carried out under the leadership of a mass political organization that was taking firm strides along the path the country had chosen. At a time when the population of Ghana numbered seven million, the Convention People's Party claimed a membership of over two million; for all intents and purposes, the country's entire adult population belonged to the CPP. Typically, although it did not have any organizations in the army, the CPP went so far as to establish its branches in churches. The start of this campaign was announced in 1961. At that time a party spokesman declared that "the formation of party branches in churches will help to chase away unnecessary suspicions, promote peace and happiness in Ghana, and forever stabilize the churches ... as an important wing in Ghana's move to create work and happiness."[1]

In describing the party's structure Nkrumah said that it was "built up from our own experiences, conditions, environments and concepts, entirely Ghanaian and African in outlook, and based on the Marxist socialist philosophy and worldview. Our party is likened to a tree – a huge and mighty tree with great branches sticking out everywhere." The CPP, or rather, the party's functionaries, were assigned the role of the trunk while "the four great branches of the Convention People's Party, namely the Trade Union Congress, the United Ghana Farmers' Council, the National Co-operative Council and the National Council of Ghana Women, are a composite part of the Convention People's Party. That is to say they are integral elements of the party ... "[2] All the members of these organizations received CPP membership cards. Subsequently Ghana's Young Pioneers were made part of the party structure. This type of party structure featuring collective membership was not invented by the Ghanian leadership. The British Labour Party is organised on the same principle. This is not to say, however, that the CPP was an exact copy of the Labour Party: African institutions influenced this party structure, as a result of which there arose a new type of party organization possessing both traditional and modern socio-political elements. In large part the fact that the party leader's power and prestige were secured in the party rules can be traced to traditional African social structures.

---

[1]Quoted in: *Ghana and Nkrumah*, p. 71.

[2]*Revolutionary Path*, p. 168.

After the January 1964 referendum, Ghana became a one-party state. Thus was actualized Kwame Nkrumah's conviction that the multi-party system, an institution of bourgeois democracy, was inappropriate to the African countries, given their history, and even less appropriate to any country which had declared its goal to be the building of a socialist society. "A people's parliamentary democracy with a one-party system," he wrote, "is better able to express and satisfy the common aspirations of a nation as a whole, than a multi-party parliamentary system, which is in fact only a ruse for perpetuating, and covers up, the inherent struggle between the 'haves' and 'have-nots'."[1] However, Nkrumah believed that the one-party system was not the only type of political organization the African states could employ and should exist only in those countries which had opted for socialism, as it could become a form of tyranny and despotism in conservative states.

One of the important problems of revolutionary-democratic theory and practice is the question of the party's guiding role in the state and its relationship to the state apparatus. Like all revolutionary democrats, Kwame Nkrumah advocated party leadership of the state. However, for him the fact that the party had the supreme role signified that all state organs should be subordinated to the CPP. Nkrumah made no distinction between party and state functions. "The Convention People's Party is Ghana, and Ghana is the Convention People's Party,"[2] he repeatedly declared. In actual fact, however, the state apparatus was subordinated not so much to the party, which, for a variety of reasons, was incapable of fulfilling its guiding role, as to the party leadership. All of the key posts in the state apparatus were held by party officials who reported directly to Nkrumah. Nevertheless, this did not ensure even an elementary degree of loyalty from most of them. The equation and fusing of party and state organs was fraught with great danger. It led to the substitution of party organs for organs in the state apparatus, the bureaucratization of the party apparatus and, eventually, to the weakening of the party's role as political leader.

Kwame Nkrumah declared that "Ghana's economic independence and the objective of socialism cannot be achieved without decisive party leadership".[3] This kind of leadership is indeed key to mobilizing efforts

---

[1] *Conciencism...*, pp. 100-101.

[2] *I Speak of Freedom*, p. 209.

[3] *Africa Must Unite*, p. 128.

aimed at effecting a progressive restructuring of society. But in this case it should represent a cohesive organization of people united by a single idea, an organization which relies on the whole party in its work and draws the people with it. In Ghana, however, the top party and state officials were, for the most part, indifferent to Nkrumah's socio-economic policies while some took a hostile attitude towards them. These were unprincipled people who used their position in the party to enrich themselves. Corruption and careerism flourished in the ranks of the party leadership. Kwame Nkrumah, who lived very plainly, was surrounded by people who not only did not share his asceticism but who made no attempt to conceal their wealth – believing that it was a reward they deserved for their participation in the struggle for independence. This type of conduct on the part of the party elite led the Ghanian masses to take a passive and sceptical attitude towards socialist slogans.

Nkrumah recognized that "a new revolution" was needed but he did not know how to bring it about. Speaking to the nation in his famous April 1961 Dawn Broadcast, Nkrumah voiced concern at the appearance of a new bourgeoisie that strove to use the party apparatus to further its own selfish aims.[1] The time of the broadcast underscored the gravity of the situation and the importance of the speech. For centuries the traditional rulers of the Gold Coast had made special announcements to their subjects early in the morning.

However, the measures that were taken were by no means radical. Party members were forbidden to own more than two houses and two cars. Nkrumah did not dare to thoroughly cleanse the party ranks of reactionary elements, although the situation demanded it, as he feared that those who were expelled would then oppose the government. This, for Nkrumah, was inadmissible as, according to the concept of "African socialism," there should be a universal harmony of interests and a smoothing over of contradictions when building the new society.

In this situation a decisive role could have been played by the party's left-democratic wing which had the Ideological Institute at Winneba and *The Spark* newspaper as its unofficial headquarters. The articles published in *The Spark* made extensive use of Marxist terminology and discussed the important problems facing the African revolution. But the radical activists' arguments over theory were largely scholastic, for they did not determine party policy. On the one hand, this situation reflected

[1]*Revolutionary Path,* pp. 153-159.

their organizational weakness while, on the other, it stemmed from the fact that Nkrumah did not completely share their views.

The problem of reorganizing Africa's mass national democratic parties into vanguard parties whose mission it would be to lead the fight for the socialist orientation was placed in all its urgency before that continent's progressive forces by the negative outcome of the party-building process in Ghana. Parties of this type should rely on well defined social forces which have an objective interest in seeing the country follow the non-capitalist path. These forces are primarily represented by the politically conscious workers and peasants. The necessity of creating vanguard parties in countries oriented towards socialism is recognized by the majority of African revolutionary democrats. However, just the first steps are now being taken toward creating such parties. This is related to a number of difficulties of primarily an objective nature. Given the socio-economic and educational backwardness of African countries, the task of getting workers and peasants involved in political life is still on the agenda. A vanguard party cannot be created by proclamation. Its formation should be the result of internal social, economic and political processes. As Lenin said, "one party cannot be 'transformed' into another ... A mere change of signboards is harmful and dangerous."[1] The revolutionary democrats of Africa are faced with the task of educating working men and women politically, of encouraging, not restraining, their initiative. But the difficulties hindering the creation of genuine vanguard parties do not remove the question of their formation from the current agenda. This process is now underway in countries like Angola, Mozambique, Ethiopia and the Congo.

It is interesting to note that Kwame Nkrumah, too, made several attempts to form an intra-party political vanguard. At his initiative the Vanguard Activists was created to form an organization within the CPP of activists "drawn from the most politically educated section of the Party"[2] that would consciously devote itself to the cause of socialism. This organization was charged with the task of introducing Ghana's workers and peasants to conscious political activity. This "party elite" did not become a true leader of Ghanian society, nor did it even become a link between the leadership and the rank-and-file membership because it limited itself primarily to propaganda work. Nevertheless, the mere fact

---

[1] V. I. Lenin, "Talk with a Delegation of the Mongolian People's Republic", *Collected Works,* Vol. 42, p. 361.

[2] *I Speak of Freedom,* p. 164.

that such an organization was formed indicates that not many years passed after independence was gained before Kwame Nkrumah realized that organizational changes had to be made in this mass political party.

The National Leader

As the party had not become an efficacious political organization and as the ineffective state apparatus was being eaten away by corruption and was not accomplishing the immediate tasks it had been assigned, Kwame Nkrumah tried to take upon himself the entire, enormous complex of governing, organizational and monitoring functions. The upshot of this and to some extent the reason for it was the glorification of Nkrumah. Credit for all the successes independent Ghana scored was given to the President personally. Nkrumah stood, ennobled in bronze, on pedestals. His visage adorned banknotes, coins and stamps. Streets and squares bore his name. Poems and hymns were composed in his honor. In official speeches and in the press one or more of his official titles always appeared before his name: Osagyefo (Victor), Father of the Nation, Fount of Honour, Man of Destiny, Star of Africa, Messiah . . . He was General Secretary of the CPP, Life President, Head of Government and Supreme Commander of the armed forces.

Was this the result of Kwame Nkrumah's inordinate ambition and his dictatorial aspirations, as many Western specialists on Ghana are inclined to say, or was something else behind it? The question is a difficult one but it must be posed, particularly as similar tendencies have been observed not only in Ghana during Nkrumah's tenure but in other African states as well.

It is true that Nkrumah's prestige was extremely high and that his ideas and opinions were unquestioned. To a large extent this is explained by the enormous popularity he acquired during the struggle to end colonialism. The attainment of political independence was linked in the consciousness of the people with the specific individual who had headed the liberation movement. In any weakly differentiated society where there is a low literacy rate and remnants of the patriarchal feudal system survive, an individual of this sort can become a type of "messiah" in the mass consciousness, destined to establish "a kingdom of liberty and justice." It is no accident, then, that one of Nkrumah's titles points directly to his saving mission.

As a national figure (a new phenomenon in Gold Coast politics)

Kwame Nkrumah had a position which placed him above the traditional institutions of power familiar to most people. In addition, Nkrumah became a living symbol of national unity. This strong, authoritative leader was somehow above all ethnic and tribal differences. He preached the idea of a national and African, rather than a local community. All this led to the deification of this "chief" in the minds of the illiterate masses, who were susceptible to religious prejudice. Thus, a charismatic leader was born.

Leaders of this type appeared after the Second World War when the biggest surge in the liberation struggle throughout the world occurred. To a large extent they were responsible for the success of the national liberation movement while, at the same time, that movement made them outstanding modern political figures who enjoyed enormous prestige internationally. They included Nehru, Sukarno, Nkrumah and Nasser. The anti-colonial movement was personified and viewed through the prism of the actions and ideas of its leaders. Moreover, the masses were not alone in this: it was the prevalent approach in historical and political literature.

The national liberation struggle in the Gold Coast, as in other African colonies, was waged under the banner of nationalism. And although many of the basic tenets of African nationalism had been developed before Kwame Nkrumah walked onto the political stage, it is he who made nationalism the ideology of the liberation movement and popularized it among the oppressed colonial masses. Thus, from the very beginning he was not only a political but an ideological leader of the national liberation revolution, and nationalism was personified in his personality, too.

The roots of the charismatic leader phenomenon also lie in the attitude the leaders and their closest associates took to the role the leader should play in the political life of the country. A typical statement on this point was made in the CPP organ. *The Spark:* "The charismatic personality of President Nkrumah is one of the props on which the new nation of Ghana is built. It is not one of mere personality worship. It is the most practical way of providing the new ship of state with a stable keel..."[1] This situation created an atmosphere in which glorification of Nkrumah was obligatory. It gave free rein to flattery of every kind, flattery which frequently had mercenary motivations. Here is a typical example of such excessive praise by the party functionary Tawia Adamafio: "...Kwame Nkrumah is our father, teacher, our brother, our friend, indeed our very

[1]Basil Davidson, *Black Star...*, p. 192.

lives, for without him we would no doubt have existed, but we would not have lived; here would have been no hope of a cure for our sick souls, no taste of glorious victory after a lifetime of suffering. What we owe to him is greater even than the air we breathe, for he made us as surely as he made Ghana."[1] Nkrumah himself looked with understanding on this and similar manifestations of devotion and made no effort to prevent a charismatic halo from appearing around his personality, believing that the success of his policies depended on it. As the prominent Soviet scholar R. A. Ulyanovsky has noted, "Nkrumah's many years in power accustomed the people to this personality cult while in him it fostered a desire to rule single-handedly by decree."[2]

The exaltation of Nkrumah's personality was also prompted by the fact that he found himself "one on one" with the masses. The party could not become an intermediate link as it was an amorphous mass organization whose policies were governed by Kwame Nkrumah's ideological directives. It acted primarily as a transmitter of his policies and not always a reliable one at that, as the widest possible variety of political trends, frequently running contrary to the party leader's socialist aspirations, were represented in the CPP and its leadership. As the party was in a subordinate position, its leader did not pay sufficient attention to party affairs. One observer of events in Ghana noted that "Nkrumah had little time or taste for activities and affairs. He was content to take the party's health for granted on the strength of sheafs of telegrams of felicitations and loyalty from party functionaries across the country on certain specified days in the year."[3] Vast rallies at which Nkrumah spoke constituted the main type of CPP activity involving the masses.

Given this state of affairs the party could not become the guiding force in the country, nor could it head the struggle to reorganize society on a non-capitalist basis. Nkrumah and his closest associates tried to fulfil these functions, even though the party's leading and guiding role was constantly stressed in Nkrumah's speeches and in CPP program documents. The clash of diverse social interests in the corridors of power did not lead to an open split thanks only to the personality of the leader who, up to a

---

[1]Quoted in: David Apter, *Ghana in Transition,* Princeton University Press, Princeton, N.J., 1972, pp. 325-326.

[2]R. A. Ulyanovsky, *Politicheskie portrety bortsov za natsional'nuyu nezavisimost',* Politizdat, Moscow, 1980, p. 125.

[3]Jitendra Mohan, "Nkrumah and Nkrumahism", *The Socialist Register 1967,* Merlin Press, London, 1967, p. 217.

certain point, acted as a regulator of contradictions within the party and state leadership. The "equilibrium" policy which Nkrumah pursued with regard to the various, often hostile groups, is illustrated by the make-up of the Presidential Commission he appointed to take over for him when he was abroad or ill. It was made up of a traditional chief, a senior state official and a member of the party's left wing. Given the growing social contradictions within the country and the absence of efficacious political organizations, collective leadership was impossible and the entire mechanism of power rested on an unconditional recognition of Nkrumah's authority. The party's Central Committee was not elected. Its members were appointed by Kwame Nkrumah and their names were not made public.

Nkrumah and his associates did not think it necessary to have government program discussed on a broad scale. They preferred to retain power and maintain a monopoly on the decision-making process. The activity of the masses was placed under the control of the leader and those around him who had the political initiative and "presented" the people with socio-economic gains. At the same time, they genuinely believed that this type of relationship with the people was the highest form of democracy possible under African conditions. The pursuance of an initiative-from-above policy rather than the development and consideration of the broad initiative of the working masses hindered the growth of the people's political activity and consciousness and led to the leadership's alienation from those in whose interests they attempted to act. Thus, this policy undermined the stability of Nkrumah's government.

The lessons Ghana provides are irrefutable evidence that the revolutionary process is doomed to crisis if the political mobilization of the masses to carry out progressive social reforms is not conducted on a broad scale and if these reforms do not come to concern them closely but are rather proclaimed by the group in power. The policy of "smoothing over" class antagonisms and the refusal to provide firm, principled support for genuine revolutionary forces capable of putting a stop to reaction's subversive activities if need be, creates a serious threat to the viability of any revolutionary democratic government and leads in the end to departure from the revolutionary path of struggle for social progress.

The attempts made to establish a direct leader-masses tie in Ghana and several other African countries proved futile and dangerous. In every case this policy created a gap between the leader and the people and led to the rise of a personality cult which was artificially inflated as development-related problems increased. Cut off from the masses, the political leadership became ineffective, basing its policies on abstractions to a significant degree, being unaware of the country's actual needs. This explains the tendency to neglect urgent domestic problems and the practice of giving first priority to foreign affairs. Those leaders who did not realize the seriousness of the situation in time were removed from office, while the masses passively stood by. Such was the case with Kwame Nkrumah, Modibo Keita and Ahmed Ben Bella.

The authoritative political leadership problem is exceedingly relevant to newly free nations. For a number of objective and subjective reasons, political leaders in African countries amass enormous power. Revolutionary-democratic leaders must fully utilize this power in the interests of the working masses, i.e. in the interests of the socialist transformation of society. Lenin pointed to the real possibility of such a situation arising: "That in the history of revolutionary movements the dictatorship of individuals was very often the expression, the vehicle, the channel of the dictatorship of the revolutionary classes has been shown by the irrefutable experience of history."[1] However, this dictatorship, which Lenin characterized as the subordination of the will of thousands "to the will of one",[2] must not be confused with personality cults and personal power regimes such as took shape in Ghana under Nkrumah and in several other African countries. Phenomena of this type occurred precisely because this subordination did not exist and because there was a gap between the "thousands" and the "one" on top.

Even if the personal power system is personified in a leader who is devoted to the cause of the revolution and who strives to govern his country in the interests of the people, it has serious negative consequences for the revolutionary process. It inevitably leads to the leadership's isolation from the social base of progressive reforms, reduces the independence of the working masses, hinders the development of their initiative and engenders political indifference. These anti-democratic processes are incompatible with the basic tenets of the socialist orientation. One of the main tasks now facing revolutionary-democratic leaders is the elimination and avoidance of these negative phenomena.

After the coup in Ghana, many revolutionary-democratic leaders drew the appropriate conclusions. Most of them set about politicizing the

[1] V. I. Lenin, "The Immediate Tasks of the Soviet Government", *Collected Works*, Vol. 27, p. 267.
[2] Ibid., p. 269.

working masses, strengthening the party's guiding role, cleansing it of hostile and chance elements and pursuing more sober and realistic domestic and foreign policies. These conclusions enriched Africa's revolutionary-democratic thought, helped strengthen progressive regimes and enabled them to make effective use of advantages offered by the socialist orientation. On the other hand, in those countries where the lessons Ghana provided were not given sufficient attention or the wrong conclusions were drawn, the socialist orientation was threatened. That is why the creation of an effective leadership and a genuine organization of people united by a single idea – the socialist future of their country – retains its importance. In this context it is appropriate to recall Lenin's words: "No revolutionary movement can endure without a stable organization of leaders maintaining continuity ... the broader the popular mass drawn spontaneously into the struggle, which forms the basis of the movement and participates in it, the more urgent the need for such an organization ... "[1]

[1]V. I. Lenin, "What Is to Be Done?", *Collected Works,* Vol. 5, p. 464.

VIII. Reinterpretation

Kwame Nkrumah was going through a difficult period in his life. He suffered attacks of melancholy more and more often and made fewer and fewer public appearances. Once he had derived great pleasure from meeting and talking with people. Now he preferred to spend his time alone in the quiet of his office. His entourage spoke of how the country was flourishing, of universal happiness and love for the Father of the Nation. He believed what he heard because he wanted to believe it. But, when he was alone once more, Nkrumah could not shake the feeling that the situation in the country had little in common with the official reports while his theories had never been farther from realization. The single vast picture he had once had of an "African type" of socialist society built through industrialization, agricultural cooperation and a return to the wellsprings of traditional humanism was by now broken up into numerous separate fragments and attempts to put them together resulted in strange and frightening combinations.

The unending attempts on Nkrumah's life were convincing proof that the army and the police could no longer be fully trusted. The last attempt was made on January 2, 1964. A policeman fired five shots at Nkrumah as he walked from his official residence to his car. The President was unhurt and he even helped disarm the assailant but one of his bodyguards was killed. Kwame Nkrumah had never felt so alone. He retreated further and further into himself, associating with only a small group of people, and increasingly left the day-to-day business of running the country to others. Nkrumah had always tried personally to direct all the processes occurring within the country. That had turned out to be impossible and now they were out of his control altogether. Incessantly rising prices, industrial strikes, increasing corruption in the state and party apparatus and rumblings of discontent within the army defined Ghana's political climate in late 1965 and early 1966. The present no longer inspired Nkrumah, so he tried to find solace in the past. Surrounding himself with books and notes, he worked on a basic history of Africa.

The only area in which Kwame Nkrumah continued to feel confident of his powers was foreign affairs. Here, he still had not tasted the full bitterness of disappointment, despite the obvious but, as he thought, temporary setback he had experienced in attempting to create a close political alliance of independent African states. His great international prestige and his position as one of the leaders of the non-aligned movement obliged him to take an active part in world affairs. Continuing to believe in the "third force" and the special role Africa was destined to play in the achievement of a universal peace, Nkrumah decided to visit the Democratic Republic of Vietnam, against which the U.S. government was conducting massed aerial warfare. From there he planned to go to the United States. Having determined the position of all the parties which had been drawn into the conflict, he would take on the role of mediator and try to bring about peace. The President of Ghana sent a message to U.S. President Lyndon Johnson, asking him to halt the bombing of Hanoi, at least for the duration of his visit. In his answer Johnson promised to do so and asked Nkrumah "to tell Hanoi that our military resistance would end when the aggression ends."[1] This monstrous cynicism clearly indicated what position U.S. leaders took on the matter but Nkrumah did not lose hope of conducting a successful peace mission.

On February 21, 1966 foreign diplomats and Ghanian officials saw Nkrumah and the delegation of over 80 persons who accompanied him off at the airport in Accra. The situation in the country was uneasy. Those close to the President advised him not to leave the country and warned him that there was danger of a coup. Nkrumah could not quite believe that there was a possibility he might be deposed. He knew there were forces that savagely opposed him and he thought that he might be killed one day but a coup d'état seemed unrealistic. He counted on the love the people had for the Father of the Nation, on the people who would not let anyone govern them other than the man they had elected. Waving goodbye to those who had come to see him off, Nkrumah disappeared into the plane. It was the last time he saw Ghana.

On the night of February 23, when Kwame Nkrumah was high in the air, bound for a stop in Peking on his way to Hanoi, a group of army officers

[1]*Ghana and Nkrumah,* p. 102.

led by Lieutenant-General Joseph Ankrah – who had been discharged from the army not long before – carried out a coup d'état that had been planned far in advance. A garrison quartered in Tamale had been brought to Accra in lorries. Most of the soldiers came from the backward Northern Territories. Therefore, they were illiterate and had little understanding of politics. They were told that Nkrumah planned to send them to fight in Vietnam, and that was the reason he had gone there, taking eight million pounds sterling with him. Beyond giving these soldiers their orders, the officers explained to them that they had been granted the great honor of reestablishing law and order in the country.

By 5 a.m. on February 24 the rebels had seized a radio station. One of the leaders of the coup, Colonel Emmanuel Kwasi Kotoka, went on the air to announce that, acting in concert, the military and the police had overthrown the government, dissolved Parliament and deposed Kwame Nkrumah. Henceforth the Convention People's Party was banned. The population of Accra took this news – which only yesterday had been inconceivable – calmly. However, shots were heard near Flagstaff House, the residence of the deposed president. Inside, a small band of guards (around 30 persons), loyal to the oath they had sworn, tried to hold off the troops who surrounded the building. By 10:30, though, the resistance had been quelled. Soldiers stupefied by alcohol and hashish burst into the house and went to work destroying anything and everything. They attacked the books in Nkrumah's extensive library with particular frenzy, ripping them apart and trampling them under their boots.

Now the military and the police were in complete control. They began to arrest ministers, members of Parliament and CPP activists. Nkrumah's wife and children were sent to Cairo. His mother, who lived in Flagstaff House, was thrown out onto the street and later sent to Nkroful.

By this time Nkrumah had landed in Peking. At the airport he was met by Zhou Enlai and other Chinese officials. News of the coup had already reached Peking but those who had come to welcome Nkrumah decided that informing him of it would not be the best way to greet their African guest. Later the Chinese Ambassador to Ghana told Nkrumah, who was resting after his long flight, of the events of the previous night. Contrary to expectation, Nkrumah took the news relatively calmly. He was neither angry nor depressed. Summoning the delegation he informed them that they must return to Ghana immediately to put down the rebellion. Speaking from the Ghanaian Embassy on February 25, Nkrumah declared, "I am the constitutional head of the Republic of Ghana, and the Commander-in-chief of the armed forces...I know that the Ghanaian people are always loyal to me . . . "[1] He ordered the soldiers who had taken part in the rebellion to return to their barracks. The Ghanian embassies were directed to send all communications and documents not to Accra, but to the Ghanian Embassy in Peking.

The news from Ghana, however, was not encouraging. The mass demonstrations of protest against the usurpers that Nkrumah anticipated did not take place, and the military had no intention of returning to their barracks. Once they had set up the National Liberation Council which appropriated legislative and executive power they exercised complete control over the situation in Ghana. The head of the Council, Lieutenant-General Joseph Ankrah, announced that the armed forces had overthrown the government in accordance with "the oldest and most treasured tradition of the people of Ghana, the tradition that a leader who loses the confidence and support of his people and resorts to the arbitrary use of power should be deposed."[2] Many of Nkrumah's closest and seemingly most reliable companions-in-arms turned against their leader. At a press conference after the coup one of Nkrumah's political protégés, Kofi Baako, declared that it had always "pained" him to realise that "Nkrumah was not a genuine leader." The President's advisor on African affairs, Michael Dei-Anang, also "realized" immediately after the coup that Nkrumah had been pursuing a "bankrupt policy on African unity" and was "a political incubus."[3] The members of the delegation accompanying Kwame Nkrumah on his trip used various excuses to desert him and return to Ghana in order to demonstrate their loyalty to the new government.

Returning to Ghana was now out of the question. Nkrumah accepted Ahmed Sékou Touré's invitation to go to Guinea. On March 2 he arrived in Conakry together with his bodyguards and the few civil servants who had remained with him. There Nkrumah was received as a head of state and given a 21-gun salute. At the airport Touré declared that Kwame Nkrumah would become, with him, "the head of state of Guinea and secretary general of the Guinean Democratic Party."[4] At a rally in

[1]Kwame Nkrumah, *Dark Days in Ghana,* International Publishers, New York, 1968, pp. 10, 11.

[2]Quoted in: Kwesi Armah, *Ghana: Nkrumah's Legacy,* p. 81.

[3]T. Peter Omari, *Kwame Nkrumah. The Anatomy of an African Dictatorship,* C. Hurst & Co., London, 1970, pp. 6-7.

[4]Quoted in: *Ghana and Nkrumah,* p. 117.

Conakry later in the day Nkrumah declared: "I have come here purposely to use Guinea as a platform to tell the world that very soon I shall be in Accra, in Ghana."[1]

Kwame Nkrumah took up residence in the Guinean capital, in a well-guarded villa situated near the ocean. The precautionary measures were by no means unnecessary. The new, self-appointed rulers of Ghana announced that a reward of 100,000 cedi or $120,000 was being placed on the former President's head. The villa was fairly spacious but almost the only room Nkrumah used was the study. There he spent a great deal of time reading the latest books on political and social history and philosophy. He studied the works of Marx, Engels and Lenin with particular care. It was at this time that Nkrumah realized how little he knew of that great teaching and what a superficial grasp he had of some of its tenets.

Visitors were frequent: foreign diplomats accredited in Guinea, prominent members of the African national liberation movement, old friends and companions-in-arms from many countries, Ghanaian emigrants and Guinean leaders. Sékou Touré and his wife often came to see him. The point of all these visits was by no means just to cheer up the influential exile. During many of them Africa's present and future were heatedly discussed. Nkrumah was asked for his advice and his opinions were challenged. The views and plans of the pioneer of African independence, who had contributed in so many ways to theory and political practice, were of interest to many.

Kwame Nkrumah avoided the press and refused to give interviews. He rarely left the confines of his residence. True, as honorary head of state Nkrumah was always at Sékou Touré's side on Guinean national holidays. He spent the rest of his time either in his study or in the garden which surrounded the villa. Roses remained his passion. The numerous bushes with their neat labels giving the name and date of planting were an object of pride for the man who had grown them and of admiration for his guests. Sometimes he played tennis or took walks near the villa. Nkrumah also realized a long-cherished dream – to learn to speak French well enough to converse freely with representatives of French-speaking Africa. Now, as a result of persistent study, he could speak fluent French and he beamed like a diligent schoolboy when his abilities were praised.

But free time was scarce. During his first months in exile Nkrumah was confident that he would soon be returning to Ghana. Using a powerful

[1]Ibid.

transmitter, he frequently spoke to his people, explaining the pro-imperialist nature of the military putsch and calling on them to "prepare to revolt against the clique of oppressive and deceiving adventurers."[1] In his first address, made ten days after the coup and timed to coincide with the ninth anniversary of Ghana's independence, Nkrumah said in a deliberately calm and firm voice: "I know that you are always loyal to me, the Party and the Government and I expect you all at this hour of trial to remain firm in determination and resistance despite intimidation . . . What has taken place in Ghana is not a coup d'état but a rebellion and it shall be crushed by its own actions . . . Very soon I shall be with you again."[2]

Later, when it became clear that the struggle would last longer than had appeared to be the case earlier, Kwame Nkrumah devoted himself entirely to theoretical work. Plainly, a significant portion of his theses had not stood the test of time. Moreover, he saw a great many things differently now.

In exile he wrote a series of major works in which he attempted to interpret events occurring, primarily, in Africa: *Dark Days in Ghana, Challenge of the Congo, Handbook of Revolutionary Warfare,* and a book with the noteworthy title *Class Struggle in Africa.* From these works it is clear that Nkrumah's views on the basic questions of the African revolution were undergoing significant alteration. At times they directly contradicted opinions he had held earlier. This is true above all of the way he looked at traditional African society, classes and class contradictions and the forms of struggle appropriate to Africa's restructuring along socialist lines. Apparently, the radical changes that occurred in Nkrumah's political and philosophical creed were not just a reaction to the coup in Ghana. Nkrumah had reached many of these conclusions during the final years of his presidency but political inertia, a reluctance to demolish Nkrumahism, which had been widely popularized, and, finally, a simple lack of time had not allowed him to give expression in theory to the changes which had occurred in his ideological views. In exile he had a chance to stop and look at events in Ghana and Africa in a new way. Kwame Nkrumah's opinions are of considerable interest since he was one of the most important theoreticians of the African national liberation movement and was highly esteemed by the revolutionary forces of that continent.

[1]Quoted in: *Ghana and Nkrumah,* p. 117.
[2]*Revolutionary Path,* pp. 391, 393.

First of all, Kwame Nkrumah came to believe that the party must be rebuilt at the stage of non-capitalist development. He admitted that the CPP had been "a compromise organization" and that there had been a large group of people within it who were interested in independence only insofar as it benefited them. Nevertheless, Nkrumah had given them important appointments, bringing them into the government in the hope that they "would act honestly and would assist to build the state on a new basis."[1] Time showed the illusionary nature of these hopes.

In this period Nkrumah became completely convinced of the need to create within the framework of the party a narrower, vanguard association to be made up of advocates of the socialist orientation who would direct the transformation of society. The coup, he wrote, had taught the CPP an important lesson as it showed that the old organization had been imperfect and that it was impossible to rely on a broad coalition of interests. Rather, a new type of leadership had to be created which would come from among the broad masses. "... Socialism cannot be achieved without socialists..."[2], i.e. without a political organization of like-minded people, he concluded.

The reactionary coup, which had not only received active support from the bureaucratic bourgeoisie but had been engendered, to no small extent, by the actions of this class, clearly showed where attempts to employ an "Africanized" colonial state apparatus in the interests of progressive development can lead. After analyzing his lack of success in employing old norms of state law Kwame Nkrumah concluded that any national-democratic state wishing to defend and extend its revolutionary gains must make the system of state organs and institutions national in character. This is accomplished not by a mechanical type of "Africanization" but through political education effected in the spirit of the nation's interests. In *Dark Days in Ghana* he said: "after a people's revolution it is essential that the top ranks of the Armed Forces, Police and Civil Service be filled by men who believe in the ideology of the Revolution, and not by those whose loyalties remain with the old order."[3]

From the very first it was clear to Kwame Nkrumah that a connection existed between the coup and the activities of U.S. intelligence services in his country. Simple logic alone suggested who benefited by the over-

---

[1] *Dark Days in Ghana,* p. 71.
[2] Ibid., p. 79.
[3] Ibid., p. 67.

throw of the anti-imperialist government. Moreover, even before the coup Nkrumah had received reports of increased activity on the part of CIA residents in Ghana. At the time he did not attach much importance to this. In exile, everything fell into place. "It has been one of the tasks of the C.I.A. and other similar organisations," he wrote, "to discover... potential quislings and traitors in our midst, and to encourage them by bribery and the promise of political power, to destroy the constitutional government of their countries."[1] At that time many people in the West were inclined to view this as the political rhetoric of a deposed president. Later, when a few U.S. intelligence service documents and the confession of some CIA employees became public, it was definitively established that CIA agents had maintained extremely close ties with the conspirators at the time the plans for the coup were being made, and that these agents monitored and directed the officers' actions. Involvement by "quiet Americans" in the counterrevolutionary action of February 23 is also indicated by the fact that Howard T. Banes, the CIA station chief in Accra at the time, received a big promotion immediately after the coup and eventually became chief of operations for the African desk at that organization's Washington headquarters.[2]

However, it should be noted that even after the coup Nkrumah was unable to assess Ghana's socioeconomic and political development prior to 1966 in a scientific and truly self-critical way. Limiting himself to an acknowledgement of a few, by then completely obvious mistakes in the area of party and state building, he did not go one step further and thoroughly analyze all of the internal factors which had led to the country's departure from the progressive path of development and, to a certain extent, to the discrediting of the socialist orientation policy in the form in which it had existed in Ghana. As he hoped to be returned to power soon, Nkrumah apparently did not think it necessary to heap criticism on the basic tenets of his domestic policy, particularly as there was no lack of criticism from either the left or the right at the time. In his books, articles and speeches he emphasized the obvious successes the country had scored in the economy, science and culture under his leadership. From the standpoint of short-term strategy this approach may have been justified. However, a sober analysis of the various reasons for the negative trends in Ghana's non-capitalist development and of his own

[1]Ibid., p. 49.
[2]*New York Times,* May 9, 1978, p. 6.

mistakes, done by the man who bore the main burden of responsibility for that country's fate, would have contributed a great deal to the theory and practice of the national liberation movement. It would also have been highly instructive for that continent's other revolutionaries.

Nkrumah had always been drawn to major theoretical problems and it was on them that he decided to focus his attention while in exile. A great deal of space in his works is given to the questions of class structure and class struggle in Africa. His views on these problems, which previously had not existed for him, underwent profound alteration. First, he renounced what had once been fundamental to his world outlook – the view that traditional African society was classless and characterised by an egalitarian humanism. He argued against idealizing or making a fetish of this society. Colonialism, he wrote, "was not preceded by an African Golden Age" and traditional African society "was neither classless nor devoid of a social hierarchy."[1] Colonial subjugation, he maintained, had created a situation wherein "the economies of the colonies became interconnected with world capitalist markets. Capitalism, individualism, and tendencies to private ownership grew."[2]

These and similar statements demonstrate that Kwame Nkrumah was already taking a more scientific approach to the study of traditional society. That his views had developed in a positive direction was also borne out by the fact that he subjected the "African socialism" concept to criticism, calling it "meaningless and irrelevant."[3] "The myth of African socialism is used," he maintained, "to deny the class struggle, and to obscure genuine socialist commitment. It is employed by those African leaders who are compelled – in the climate of the African Revolution – to proclaim socialist policies, but who are at the same time deeply committed to international capitalism, and who do not intend to promote genuine socialist economic development."[4]

The logical step to take after such sharp criticism of "national" socialism, a concept he himself had advocated until quite recently, was to recognise Marxism-Leninism as the only scientific theory capable of explaining Africa's past and present and outlining its future. Kwame Nkrumah took that

[1] *Revolutionary Path,* pp. 440, 441.
[2] *Class Struggle in Africa,* p. 14.
[3] Ibid., p. 26.
[4] Ibid.

step. "There is only one true socialism and that is scientific socialism,"[1] he declared. This conclusion constitutes the main result of Nkrumah's ideological evolution, his political testament to the revolutionary forces of the African continent. Admittedly, Kwame Nkrumah had used the term scientific socialism before, when he was in power, but at the time had meant something quite different by it. *That* "scientific socialism" was Nkrumahism and its "scientific" nature was reflected in the emphasis placed on specific national features. In exile, Nkrumah declared the principles of scientific socialism to be "abiding and universal"[2] for all countries and peoples without exception. While continuing to speak of the need to bear specific national features in mind, he now warned that there could be "no compromise over socialist goals."[3]

Nkrumah's Class Analysis

Having previously rejected the idea that African society was divided into classes Nkrumah now came to recognize the existence of classes in Africa as well as of class struggle. This change in his thinking was not the end product of abstract meditation. Rather, it was prompted by specific events on the continent. The exacerbation of class antagonisms throughout Africa together with the counterrevolutionary coups in Ghana and Mali offered clear proof that movement forward along the path of social progress would not occur if based on the concept of "class harmony." In his book devoted to the class struggle in Africa, Kwame Nkrumah said: "At the core of the problem is the class struggle ... Class divisions in the modern African society became blurred to some extent during the pre-independence period, when it seemed there was national unity and all classes joined forces to eject the colonial power. This led some to proclaim that there were no class divisions in Africa ... But the exposure of this fallacy followed quickly after independence when class cleavages, temporarily submerged in the struggle to win political freedom, reappeared ... in those states where the newly independent government embarked on socialist policies."[4] This serious scientific conclusion

[1]Kwame Nkrumah, *Handbook of Revolutionary Warfare,* International Publishers, New York, 1969, p. 29.

[2]Ibid.

[3]*Class Struggle in Africa,* p. 26.

[4]*Class Struggle in Africa,* p. 10.

clearly contradicts both Nkrumah's ideological directives and the spirit of the policies he pursued before the coup. It was, in essence, belated criticism of the mistakes he had made and an acknowledgement that his policy of "smoothing over" class antagonisms had been bankrupt.

His growing conviction that the class struggle must inevitably be exacerbated compelled Nkrumah to look at the class structure of African society and the driving forces behind the revolutionary process in Africa in a new way.

In his analysis of class structure Nkrumah did not use the term "class" in its scientific sense. As is well known the Marxist-Leninist definition of "class" is based on the objective criterion of the relation people have to the means of production. Nkrumah, however, based his definition of "class" on the concept of "interest", and did not bear in mind that the interests of different classes can coincide during certain periods of history. He maintained that classes were nothing more than the sum total of individuals united by certain interests which they, as a class, attempt to defend. This definition of class allowed the most diverse categories of people to be grouped together and thereby deprived Nkrumah's class analysis of precision. Thus, Nkrumah included peasants, small tradesmen, manual laborers and migrant workers in the working class.[1] It should be noted that in this schematization of class divisions the "working class" category does not exist. Instead, he used the term to describe people who work for a living. In his concrete class analysis Nkrumah used the term "proletariat" which corresponds more precisely to the scientific definition of the working class in Africa and takes in industrial and agricultural workers.

By the term "peasantry" Kwame Nkrumah meant all farmers who do not use hired labor on their farms. The fact that Nkrumah recognized rural class stratification and divided the rural population into exploiters and exploited is an extremely important point. He regarded the well-to-do peasants as part of the petty-bourgeoisie which, he maintained, is made up of two groups – farmers whose social status is determined by the size of their holdings and the number of hired hands they employ, and the urban petty bourgeoisie (small shopkeepers, artisans, etc.), who also are not a heterogeneous group.

Nkrumah distinguished these social strata from the "bourgeois classes' ' – the national bourgeoisie per se, compradors, entrepreneurs, and

[1] Ibid., p. 68.

"capitalism's representatives" – the professional and managerial class, etc.[1] A prominent place in his work was given to a critique of the role of the bureaucratic bourgeoisie. After revealing the close ties it has with the African exploiting classes and imperialism, and pointing to its isolation from the masses Nkrumah noted that, in general, it is "dedicated to the capitalist path of development and [is] among the most devoted of indigenous agents of neocolonialism."[2]

Kwame Nkrumah included a consideration of the traditional rulers of African society in his analysis of its classes. Without a doubt the traditional institutions of power continue to play a significant role in Africa. Feudal and tribal chiefs whose authority is based on patriarchal customs and traditions maintain a hold on the peasant masses and restrain the growth of their political consciousness to a certain degree. But no matter what social role the representatives of traditional institutions may play or political influence they may have, from the point of view of scientific socialism this is not sufficient reason to consider them a separate class. The traditional chief social group, too, contains such heterogeneous elements as feudal rulers (e.g. in northern Nigeria, northern Cameroon), who live off the peasants and are increasingly merging with the bourgeoisie, and rural chiefs, who frequently work their own plots of land and, differing hardly at all from the peasants, possess purely nominal power.

The social divisions Kwame Nkrumah discerned in African society are proof of his greater ideological and political maturity. Discarding the categories into which he had previously divided society – progressive and reactionary forces – he attempted to determine how the various classes and social groups fit into the revolutionary process. Nowhere in his works did Nkrumah use the term "the driving forces behind the revolution." Nevertheless it is clear that he assigned the main role in the African revolution to the working masses – the working class and the peasantry.

Kwame Nkrumah's assessment of the part the working class is to play in the revolutionary transformation of society deserves to be given particular attention. Nkrumah concluded that the working class should become the main force behind the revolutionary movement in Africa because it had the potential to become the foremost class in African society. At the same time he noted that the absence of highly developed industry and a low level of skill and education among workers delay the growth of

[1]*Class Struggle in Africa,* p. 20.
[2]Ibid., p. 61.

working-class consciousness. Nkrumah rejected the thesis, popular among many African ideologists, that the working class is incapable of acting as the vanguard of the revolution because it is small. "A modern proletariat already exists in Africa, though it is relatively small in size," he wrote. "This is the class base for the building of socialism... [and] it must be assessed by its performance and its potential... "[1] This statement is completely in keeping with the conclusions Marx, Engels and Lenin drew concerning the role of working class in history and its place in the revolutionary movement. As Lenin explained, "the strength of the proletariat in the process of history is immeasurably greater than its share of the total population."[2]

It is very important to note that Kwame Nkrumah recognized that the hegemony of the international working class is global in nature and encompasses those countries where the modern working class is still in the process of being formed. He saw the African proletariat not as a separate entity, but as part of the international working class movement "from which it derives much of its strength".[3] The fact that he posed the proletarian internationalism question sets Nkrumah apart, even among today's revolutionary democrats.

It is typical of Nkrumah's thinking that he did not regard the working class as an abstract category but rather examined the position and revolutionary potential of its various contingents. Emphasising that a large part of the African working class is made up of migrant and seasonal workers, he noted that if they were organized and the appropriate kind of work were done with them they "can become a vital factor in the African socialist revolution,... can be a very powerful force for the spread of revolutionary socialism"[4] due to their mobility and ties with the rural population. Involving migrant and seasonal workers in the revolutionary movement is not as simple a matter as it appeared to Nkrumah, however. It is true that when yesterday's peasants come to the city they acquire, in addition to occupational skills, the germs of political consciousness. However, it seems unlikely that they would be able to comprehend the "ideas of revolutionary socialism" given the relatively brief amount of time they spend in the city. Moreover, they are frequently the bearers of

[1]*Class Struggle in Africa,* p. 64.

[2]V. I. Lenin, "The Development of Capitalism in Russia", *Collected Works,* Vol. 3, 1977, p. 31.

[3]*Class Struggle in Africa,* p. 64.

[4]Ibid., p. 68.

archaic tribal social relations and reproduce these in the city, thus complicating the growth of working-class consciousness. However, the necessity of conducting political work among this section of Africa's working class is not in doubt.

Nor did Kwame Nkrumah ignore such a typical phenomenon as the presence in many African countries of a fairly large contingent of foreign workers. Noting that a few African regimes deliberately fan "their" workers' dissatisfaction over the "foreigners" – whom the former see as the cause of job and housing shortages as well as rising prices – he wrote that only "the bourgeoisie benefit from the split among the ranks of the working class. Workers are workers, and nationality, race, tribe and religion are irrelevancies in the struggle to achieve socialism."[1] This call for international solidarity among Africa's workers was even more timely given the fact that in several African countries, including Ghana, in the late '60s and early '70s the trend towards persecution and expulsion of immigrant workers became more pronounced.

As Kwame Nkrumah saw it, the two main tasks of the working class in the African revolution are to forge a strong alliance with the peasantry and to awaken their revolutionary consciousness. "It is the task of the African urban proletariat," he wrote, "to win the peasantry to revolution by taking the revolution to the countryside ... once both urban proletariat and peasants join forces in the struggle to achieve socialism, the African Revolution has in effect been won."[2] For Nkrumah the peasantry is the exploited section of the rural population. He thought that the working class should join forces with the poorest peasantry in order to fulfil its historical mission.

This sober evaluation of the peasantry's revolutionary potential was made at a time when it was widely held in the national liberation movement that the peasantry was the sole revolutionary force and bearer of socialist tendencies. Franz Fanon and other ideologists placed the peasantry, "which had nothing to lose," in opposition to the working class, which, in their opinion, was in a privileged position and had "everything to lose."[3] Kwame Nkrumah did not idealize the peasantry and assigned it a supporting role in the revolution. He wrote, "The peasantry can be a revolutionary

[1]*Class Struggle in Africa*, p. 86.
[2]Ibid., p. 65.
[3]Franz Fanon, *The Wretched of the Earth*, Grove Press, New York, 1968, pp. 108-109.

class if led by the urban and rural proletariat."[1] Nkrumah's formulation of what role a close alliance of workers and peasants should play in the implementation of revolutionary reforms on the African continent had an important place in his ideological evolution and in his mastery of modern scientific conclusions concerning the driving forces behind the present stage of the national liberation movement.

Recognizing the stratification of rural society into classes, Kwame Nkrumah not only divided the rural population into two categories, the exploiters and the exploited, but he singled the rural proletariat out from the latter category and made it a separate group which he called "workers in the Marxist sense of the word."[2] The fact that the poorest peasants must work for wages is naturally something they share with the working class but they are most definitely not workers in the scientific sense of the word because they occupy a completely different place in the system of social production. Despite their external proletarian traits they remain members of the small-commodity structure. Moreover, the work farm laborers do is primarily temporary and seasonal in nature. Even the poorest peasants remain members of their communities more often than not and can count on their help and support to a certain extent. This state of affairs does not promote the development of a genuinely proletarian consciousness.

Kwame Nkrumah gave a prominent place in his class analysis to the political behavior of the African bourgeoisie. The position to be taken with regard to bourgeois and petty-bourgeois elements during the process of non-capitalist development is one of the cardinal questions of revolutionary-democratic theory and practice. Nkrumah's uncritical position with regard to the Ghanian bourgeoisie was one of the primary causes of the reactionary coup. Evidently this fact explains the extremely negative approach he subsequently took to the role and place of the bourgeoisie in the national liberation revolution.

The Ghanian theoretician noted the weakness of the national bourgeoisie and its comprador, dependent nature. "Under conditions of colonialism and neocolonialism," he wrote, "it will never be encouraged sufficiently to become strong in the economic sphere ... The local bourgeoisie must always be subordinate partners to foreign capitalists. For this reason, it cannot achieve power as a class or govern ... without the political, eco-

---

[1] *Class Struggle in Africa,* p. 77.
[2] Ibid.

nomic and military support of international capitalism."[1] In and of itself this statement does not provide any grounds for objection but on the basis of this correct proposition he concluded that the bourgeoisie must be removed immediately. "The African bourgeoisie provides a bridge for continued imperialist and neocolonialist domination and exploitation. The bridge must be destroyed,"[2] he asserted. Regarding the bourgeoisie as the cause of all of Africa's troubles, Nkrumah failed to take into consideration that the contradictions that remained between it and foreign capital enabled its patriotic members to participate in the anti-imperialist struggle. Moreover, as experience has shown, those countries that have chosen the path of socialist orientation must continue to utilize domestic private capital, as the state cannot immediately occupy the commanding heights in the economy.

Kwame Nkrumah displayed even less realism in his assessment of the petty bourgeoisie, stating that "in the revolutionary struggle, no reliance can be placed on any section... of the petty bourgeoisie."[3] It is quite clear that this statement does not describe the situation in Africa today. No single progressive government can exist without the support of the petty bourgeoisie, that broad section of society which is one of the most active forces in politics. Moreover, as practice has shown, the African petty bourgeoisie is in many cases capable of leading the way to national democratic reforms. This situation will persist for a long time, as in the majority of the countries on that continent the working class has not reached the level of political maturity and organization that would permit it to take on the job of directing the process of revolutionary change.

Naturally, a differential approach to the petty bourgeoisie is needed as it is not homogeneous and its top strata (small entrepreneurs, kulaks, etc.) tend to identify with the bourgeois class both economically and ideologically. At the current stage of the national liberation movement, however, the bulk of the petty bourgeoisie has not yet exhausted its revolutionary potential. The main reason for this is the fact that it is itself exploited by foreign and domestic private interests.

Kwame Nkrumah supposed that the petty bourgeoisie's economic interests lay in the area of capitalism and were in conflict with the profound socioeconomic changes occurring in African society, a conclusion based on the incorrect assessment he had made of the petty

[1]Ibid., p. 57.
[2]Ibid., p. 85.
[3]Ibid., p. 81.

bourgeoisie's role in the national democratic revolution. In this context it would be appropriate to recall Lenin's pronouncement concerning the role these strata play: "The petty bourgeois is in such an economic position, the conditions of his life are such that he cannot help deceiving himself, he involuntarily and inevitably gravitates one minute towards the bourgeoisie, the next towards the proletariat. It is *economically impossible* for him to pursue an independent 'line'. His past draws him towards the bourgeoisie, his future towards the proletariat."[1]

Having denied the petty bourgeoisie's revolutionary potential Kwame Nkrumah declared the united anti-imperialist front tactic inappropriate to those states that have embarked on the path of progressive reforms. "Theorists arguing that proletariat and petty bourgeoisie should join together to win the peasantry, in order to attack the bourgeoisie," he wrote "ignore the fact that the petty bourgeoisie will always, when it comes to the pinch, side with the bourgeoisie to preserve capitalism."[2] What "pinch" did Nkrumah have in mind? He maintained that the national and petty bourgeoisie consistently oppose the creation of socialist states. This, then, is the root of the incorrect position Nkrumah took with regard to the various sections of the united anti-imperialist front: he had confused the goals and tasks of the various stages of the national democratic revolution.

Typically, while he was in power Nkrumah did not consider it necessary to bear the interests of the numerically strong petty bourgeoisie in mind. He regarded these strata as a rudiment of the colonial period of the country's history and therefore doomed to wither away as Ghana speedily built socialism. The absence of a positive policy on these strata cost his government dearly. It was the peasants at the markets who largely determined the Ghanian petty bourgeoisie's cast of mind. Indeed, they played an active counterrevolutionary role, although during the struggle for independence they had been unwavering in their support of the CPP.

Many of Kwame Nkrumah's ideological errors were rooted in the false assumption that by the end of the '60s Africa had entered the stage of socialist revolution. Convinced that "the African Revolution is an integral part of the world socialist revolution," Nkrumah rejected the idea that the stage of non-capitalist development is a period of general democratic and anti-imperialist change. He wrote, " 'A non-capitalist road,' pursued

[1]V. I. Lenin, "Constitutional Illusions", *Collected Works,* Vol. 25, p. 202.
[2]*Class Struggle in Africa,* p. 58.

by a 'united front of progressive forces,' as some suggest, is not even practical politics in contemporary Africa."[1] That is why Nkrumah made the struggle for socialism the first priority at the current stage of the national liberation revolution. Here, once again, we have an example of Nkrumah's revolutionary impatience and of his desire to make the future the present, thus "accelerating" the historical process. In his day Lenin cautioned against making mistakes of this sort. "It is absurd," he wrote, "to confuse the tasks and prerequisites of a democratic revolution with those of a socialist revolution, which, we repeat, differ both in their nature and in the composition of the social forces taking part in them."[2]

The extension of the class concept to all of the problems associated with the question of revolution in Africa represents a serious modification of Nkrumah's world outlook and an important step along the road of his ideological evolution. However, for Nkrumah the class struggle was primarily reflected in open clashes between, on the one hand, the oppressed classes, who have an interest in national liberation and socialism, and, on the other, imperialism and all the other forces of neocolonialism, which aspire to wipe out the gains of the African revolution. "It is only through the resort to arms," he asserted, "that Africa can rid itself once and for all of remaining vestiges of colonialism, and of imperialism and neocolonialism; and a socialist society be established in a free and united continent."[3] Kwame Nkrumah proclaimed guerilla war to be the law of revolutionary struggle, the only means of achieving the African people's social liberation.

Armed Struggle

Nkrumah was not the first to bring armed struggle to the forefront as the only effective means the African national liberation movement had of achieving its goals. A left radical ideological trend already existed in Africa at this time which absolutized force of arms and advocated using them to resolve the domestic social problems that the continent's countries faced. Its most important representatives were Franz Fanon and Ben Barka. At first Nkrumah did not share these views but by the end of the

---

[1] Ibid., p. 84.
[2] V. I. Lenin, "Socialism and the Peasantry", *Collected Works,* Vol. 9, p. 309.
[3] *Class Struggle in Africa,* p. 87.

'60s he had taken an extremely radical position on the question of how the struggle for national and social liberation should be conducted.

Absolutizing armed struggle and guerilla methods in particular, Kwame Nkrumah believed that they could and should be used not just against racist regimes but against those African states where power is in the hands of conservative, pro-imperialist forces and where the resolution of economic problems is controlled by international finance capital. As he placed the majority of African states in the latter category, a guerilla war should, he thought, be pan-African in nature. In *Revolutionary Path* he stated that "there is only one way to achieve the African revolutionary goals of liberation, political unification and socialism. That way lies through armed struggle. The time for speechifying, for conferences, for makeshift solutions and for compromise is past."[1] This "ultra-revolutionary" approach to the African national liberation movement sets Nkrumah apart from other revolutionary democrats and places him on the extreme left of political thought in Africa.

What lay behind this swift ideological about-face? Not so very long before Nkrumah had advocated non-violence and maintained that socialism could be built by effecting insignificant reforms of African society. Now he contended that an African guerilla war was necessary if socialist aims were to be achieved. Without question, Nkrumah's radicalism was triggered by the coup in Ghana, which had been organized by internal reaction with the backing of international imperialism, a coup which had reduced him from a position as one of the leaders of the anti-imperialist movement in Africa to that of political émigré. It was, in a way, an emotional reaction to the collapse of the ideological and political theory which had taken him so long to craft and in accordance with which harmony among the classes was essential to achieving socialism in Africa. Personal experience having demonstrated this theory's bankruptcy, Nkrumah went to the opposite extreme. In exile, unable to participate in politics, he seems to have lost his sense of perspective with respect to the African revolution's future. Abandoning his efforts to find solutions to the complex problems which faced the national liberation movement in Africa, he began working out grandiose but unrealistic tactical plans.

Upon closer examination Nkrumah's "new" theory of revolution turns out to be far from original. It bears the marks of a wide range of radical left ideas popular both in the newly free nations and in developed Western countries. The "Guinean period" of Nkrumah's theoretical work

[1]*Revolutionary Path,* pp. 422–423.

coincided with the spread of various ultra-leftist ideas and theories throughout the world in the second half of the '60s. They were stimulated by a variety of factors, the most important of which was the growing involvement in the anti-imperialist movement of broad, non-proletarian masses from both the national liberation movement zone and capitalist countries. The steady rise in imperialism's aggressiveness, combined with the revelation that it was unable to suppress the popular struggle for freedom and independence by force (such was the case in Southeast Asia, Cuba, Algeria and Portugal's African colonies), gave rise to a number of ultra-revolutionary theories. In essence these declared that the victory over imperialism was near and guerilla warfare was the most appropriate means of achieving it.

Nkrumah's theory of armed popular struggle is similar to analogous theories by the main radical left ideologists on a number of basic points. Nkrumah was in sympathy with Régis Debray's assertation that "what had been a national-popular insurrection gradually became transformed into an armed socialist revolution"[1] and particularly Che Guevara's postulate that "it is not always necessary to wait for all the conditions for revolution to exist – the insurrectionary focal point can at times create them . . . "[2]

Without a doubt, the work of radical left ideologists influenced Nkrumah's thinking. To give just two examples, in his works he cites Fanon's *The Wretched of the Earth,* calling it a "specific case study of the problems of decolonization,"[3] and quotes Che Guevara. Nkrumah does not appear to have borrowed these radical ideas. Rather, we seem to be looking at a similar type of socio-psychological thinking. Instead of carefully considering specific historical situations, the former President of Ghana, like many other non-proletarian revolutionaries, preached the idea that revolution hinges on volitional factors. The subjectivism of their approach to historical processes led them to believe that the restructuring of social reality is dependent upon the wishes of the individual.

In criticizing subjective sociology, which based its theory on the efforts of the individual, Lenin wrote: "Subjective sociologists rely on arguments such as – the aim of society is to benefit all its members, that justice, therefore, demands such and such an organization, and that a system that

---

[1] Regis Debray, *The Revolution on Trial. A Critique of Arms,* Vol. 2, Penguin Books, Ltd., Harmondsworth, 1978, p. 34.

[2] *"Che" Guevara on Revolution. A Documentary Overview,* Jay Mallin, ed., University of Miami Press, Coral Gables, Florida, 1969, p. 89.

[3] *Revolutionary Path,* p. 435.

is out of harmony with this ideal organization . . . is abnormal and should be set aside. . . . From the standpoint of this sociologist there can be no question of regarding the development of society as a process of natural history."[1] The objective prerequisites for direct struggle, not to mention armed struggle, and for the socialist reconstruction of society do not, as yet, exist in Africa. The struggle to bring about political and socioeconomic change that will eliminate backwardness and pave the way for socialism is the order of the day.

The mistake Kwame Nkrumah and the other radical left ideologists make is that they suppose revolution to be born out of "popular war." In his day G. V. Plekhanov noted that people who absolutize violence argue that "as there is violence in every revolution, violent means are all that is necessary to either spark or accelerate a revolution."[2] Like Fanon before him, Nkrumah supposed that armed struggle would "incidentally" make it possible to accomplish such tasks as the political education of the masses, their organization, and spiritual emancipation. For them violence was an agent that would clear away the filth of degradation and slavery.

Nkrumah's theory of "popular war" had both military and political components. In contrast to Fanon, for example, who conceived of revolutionary violence as an explosion of peasant indignation which then grew into popular armed struggle, Nkrumah introduced elements of pan-African organization to the guerilla war. In order to coordinate an armed struggle throughout the continent, he proposed that an "All-African People's Revolutionary Army" and an "All-African People's Revolutionary Party" be created. It is quite clear that organization of this kind cannot be set up given current African conditions. Moreover, attempts to do so would further complicate efforts to strengthen that continent's unity in the face of imperialism. Given the system of nation-states that has taken shape in Africa, calls for armed struggle against existing regimes and attempts to "accelerate" the revolutionary process could cause the national liberation movement tremendous harm.

Because he did not have a genuinely scientific understanding of social processes, Nkrumah approached several modern-day problems in an oversimplified manner. This was primarily true of problems related to the

---

[1]V. I. Lenin, "What the 'Friends of the People' Are and How They Fight the Social-Democrats", *Collected Works,* Vol. 1, p. 137.

[2]G. V. Plekhanov, "Sila i nasilie", *Sochineniya,* ("Force and Violence", *Works*) Vol. 4, p. 252.

working class movement in capitalist countries. "The tendency in the transitional period between capitalism and socialism is embourgeoisement" [of the working class], he wrote. "In these conditions the worker becomes a well-fed Philistine and turns towards reaction and conservatism."[1] Thus, Nkrumah explained the defeat of the revolutionary actions in France in 1968 by the spread of bourgeois tendencies in the working class. This failure to understand the vanguard role the working class of the developed capitalist countries plays in the struggle for democratic change and socialism – the second most important revolutionary force today – is characteristic of petty bourgeois radicalism. Nkrumah appears to have directly borrowed this fallacious idea which is the cornerstone of New Left doctrine. When Nkrumah accused the working class in the West of degenerating under bourgeois influence, he was doing nothing more than repeating Marcuse's assertion that in the developed capitalist countries, characterized by an increased rate of scientific and technological progress and a relatively high standard of living, the working class was integrated into the "consumer society," lost its revolutionary potential and was changed from the antagonist into the defender of the bourgeois system.[2]

Thus, having denied that the working class in developed capitalist countries has revolutionary potential, Kwame Nkrumah assigned the principal role in the fight against imperialism and for social change to the "underprivileged" peoples of the "third world." "While conditions of embourgeoisement exist among the working class of capitalist countries," he wrote, "an added responsibility rests on the exploited peoples of Africa, Asia and Latin America to promote the world's socialist revolution."[3] Once again Nkrumah was placing tasks before the national liberation movement that it is not capable of accomplishing at this stage. It goes without saying that the national liberation movement in the developing countries is an important part of the world revolutionary movement, but in the countries where the bourgeoisie hold sway the direct struggle against imperialism and for a radical restructuring of society is being waged by the working class with the full support of the world socialist system. The national liberation movement is a powerful ally in this struggle. It undermines imperialism's position throughout the world, but in and of itself it will not eradicate the socio-economic causes of

---

[1] *Class Struggle in Africa*, p. 73.
[2] See Herbert Marcuse, *An Essay on Liberation*, Beacon Press, Boston, 1969, pp. 14-15.
[3] *Class Struggle in Africa*, p. 74.

imperialism. No matter what the subjective aspirations of their authors, concepts which absolutize the role played by the struggle of oppressed peoples are objectively aimed at isolating the national liberation movement from the other contingents of the world revolutionary movement, and this, in practice, reduces the anti-imperialist struggle's effectiveness.

There is no question that Nkrumah was influenced by Western radical left ideology. Matters are more complicated in regard to the influence the ultra-leftist, opportunistic ideas promoted by China's Maoist leadership had on his thinking. Clearly, a few Maoist theories had a certain attractiveness for those politicians who suffered from revolutionary impatience and had received poor ideological and theoretical training. Chinese theories concerning the "third world's" special mission, "the superiority of man over machine," the subjective factor's priority over the objective factor and Mao's thesis that "the poorer a people is, the more revolutionary it is" gained currency among the ideologists of developing nations. As several of his last works reveal, Kwame Nkrumah agreed with some of these theories. But their popularity in the national liberation movement is explained not by their source but first and foremost by the fact that they arose and then gained currency in a similar social milieu, characterised by underdeveloped socio-economic relations, a small, unorganized working class, the presence of petty bourgeois elements and a backward mass consciousness. The petty bourgeois nature of these theories on revolution was in keeping with the ideological aims of the subjective revolutionaries who wanted to "urge on" the revolutionary process.

The conscious use of Maoist sources can be observed in Nkrumah's writings on armed struggle. He borrowed not only ideas concerning the inevitable triumph of guerilla wars, the creation of revolutionary bases in rural areas, etc., but some Maoist terminology as well, such as "popular revolutionary war" and "paper tiger." With the exception of the general sections, Kwame Nkrumah's *Handbook of Revolutionary Warfare* clearly reveals the influence of *Selected Military Writings of Mao Tse-tung,* published in English. In attempting to set forth his "new" theory of revolution as fully as possible Nkrumah, who was not an expert on military matters, turned to the military experience of the Chinese Revolution which was distinguished by the fact that its internal and external contradictions were resolved through armed struggle. But the point is not just that Nkrumah was inclined to use the Chinese experience as the basis for his study of guerilla warfare. Aspiring to establish its hegemony over the national liberation movement, Peking universalized the Chinese experience, in part by making use of pseudo-revolutionary phraseology, and thrust it upon Africans without taking the concrete conditions of that continent into consideration. Particular danger was posed by the fact that the anti-Marxist theory of the absolute priority of armed struggle, which Chinese ideologists tried to disseminate in the newly free nations, was presented as the last word in Marxism. This compromised revolutionary ideals, played into the hands of local and international reaction and slowed the consolidation of anti-imperialist forces.

The Marxist-Leninist revolutionary teaching has always taken a creative approach to the forms of struggle for national and social liberation that may be chosen and has never absolutized any of them. The class struggle can take either a political or military form. "Marxism . . . positively does not reject any form of struggle,"[1] Lenin wrote in "Guerilla Warfare." The sovereign right of peoples everywhere to use the means they deem necessary in their struggle for liberation, violent or non-violent, has been upheld in the documents of the world communist and working class movement. However, when armed struggle is necessary, Marxists always stress that careful consideration must be given to the concrete historical situation prevailing in the country in question. Armed action must always be based on a revolutionary surge among the working masses, for without it armed action becomes a series of adventuristic and seditious acts. The absolutization of armed struggle, i.e. its proclamation as the universal method of achieving progressive goals, inflicts great harm on the national liberation movement.

When considering the effect certain Maoist ideas had on Nkrumah, it should be noted that he did not agree with the fundamental tenets of Maoist ideology or practice. Nkrumah was sharply critical of the anti-Soviet policies then pursued by the rulers of China. He regarded the Soviet Union as a trustworthy friend to all peoples who are fighting for freedom and social progress. He opposed Peking's policy of working to isolate the national liberation movement from those countries where the working class has triumphed. "The struggle against imperialism takes place both within and outside the imperialist world," he declared. "It is a struggle between socialism and capitalism, not between a so-called 'Third World' and imperialism . . . It is not possible to build socialism in the developing world in isolation from the world socialist system."[2]

Lenin's idea that the "revolutionary movement of the peoples of

[1] V. I. Lenin, "Guerilla Warfare", *Collected Works,* Vol. 11, 1972, p. 213.
[2] *Class Struggle in Africa,* p. 83.

the East can...develop effectively...only in direct association with the revolutionary struggle of our Soviet Republic against international imperialism"[1] is highly relevant in today's world. The entire course of history is convincing the members of the national liberation movement that the fundamental interests of the peoples of Asia, Africa and Latin America coincide with the interests of the countries where socialism is a reality and that closer cooperation in activating the anti-imperialist struggle is essential.

When analyzing the connection between Nkrumah's conception of the revolutionary process in Africa and the ideologies espoused by "leftist" groups in the West, the influence Nkrumah's ideas had on some of these trends should be considered. He had a particularly noticeable influence on "leftist" nationalist movements which drew their followings from among the Black population of the U.S., such as the Black Panthers and the Black Power movement.

After the explosion of actions, including advocacy of armed actions by some U.S. Black people who were fighting for their civil rights in the mid-'60s, the movement abated due to both the brutal reprisals that followed and the crisis suffered by its ideology, which was characterized by the advocacy of an isolated Black struggle. A few Black radical "left" leaders who were inspired by the impressive victories of the national liberation movement in Africa and its growing international influence, looked to it for support and hoped to make it their ally in the struggle for Black rights in the United States. There appeared theories like "neo-pan-Africanism", which in essence states that the Black population of the U.S. and the peoples of Africa constitute a single community whose national and social interests coincide. Black nationalists today see Africa as a force capable of giving new impetus to the struggle of Blacks in America. One of the founders of neo-pan-Africanism, Malcolm X, wrote: "Just as the American Jew is in harmony politically, economically, and culturally with world Jewry, it is time for all Afro-Americans to become an integral part of the world's Pan-Africanists, and even though we might remain in America physically while fighting for the benefits that the Constitution guarantees us, we must return to Africa philosophically

---

[1]V. I. Lenin, "Address to the Second All-Russia Congress of Communist Organisations of the Peoples of the East, November 22, 1919", *Collected Works,* Vol. 30, 1977, p. 151.

and culturally, and develop a working unity in the framework of Pan-Africanism."[1]

The "pan-Africanism" of which Malcolm X speaks has nothing in common with the anti-imperialist, anti-racist pan-Africanism professed by W. E. B. Du Bois throughout his life and by Nkrumah during the greater part of his. The "godfathers" of modern neo-pan-Africanism are Marcus Garvey, and, in particular, George Padmore, who tried to make the pan-African movement take an anti-communist course and isolate the struggle of oppressed peoples from the Soviet Union.

For a long time the desire to equate the struggle of Black people in the U.S. with the African national liberation movement was one-sided. Preoccupied with the numerous problems facing their own countries and their continent, African leaders did not feel an urgent need to take on the problems of the Black population in the U.S. The situation changed when Kwame Nkrumah, and after the coup proceeding from his concept of the revolutionary nature of the "underprivileged," suggested that the African revolutionary struggle "be seen in the context of the Black Revolution"[2] and announced that the liberation struggles of Blacks in Africa and America had merged into a single stream. In "The Spectre of Black Power", a chapter dedicated to Che Guevara, Ben Barka and Malcolm X he wrote: "What is Black Power? I see it in the United States as part of the vanguard of world revolution against capitalism, imperialism and neo-colonialism . . . Black Power is part of the world rebellion of the oppressed against the oppressor." Nkrumah expands the concept of Black Power and makes it global in nature. "It operates throughout the African continent, in North and South America, the Caribbean, wherever Africans and people of African descent live. It is linked with the Pan-African struggle for unity on the African continent, and with all those who strive to establish a socialist society."[3]

The support Black radical "left" nationalists received in the person of such a prominent African figure as Kwame Nkrumah gave the concept of neo-pan-Africanism added force and militancy. This support particularly inspired Stokely Carmichael, Eldridge Cleaver and James Forman. Taking Nkrumah's idea that the Blacks of the world should join forces and coordinate their strategies for "a unified armed struggle,"[4] they pro-

---

[1]Quoted in: Stokely Carmichael, *Stokely Speaks: Black Power to Pan-Africanism.* Vintage Books, New York, 1971, p. 179.

[2]*Class Struggle in Africa*, p. 87.

[3]*Revolutionary Path*, p. 426.

[4]*Revolutionary Path*, p. 427.

posed making Africa this struggle's base. Nkrumah had similar thoughts on the subject and spoke out in favor of making Africa into a national home for all blackskinned people. "The core of the Black revolution is in Africa," he wrote, "and until Africa is united under a socialist government the Black man throughout the world lacks a national home."[1] Stokely Carmichael, who called himself a disciple of Nkrumah and Nkrumah "the most brilliant man in the world today,"[2] met with him in Guinea and discussed creating a "revolutionary base" in Ghana after the lawful government had been restored.

The identification of Kwame Nkrumah with the pseudo-revolutionary Black nationalists has had some negative consequences for the African national liberation movement. Demagogically utilizing Nkrumah's prestige and a few of his ideas, the neo-pan-Africanists have increased their ideological penetration of Africa. The threat this poses does not just consist in the fact that they advocate an unrealistic policy whereby various peoples with the same color of skin are declared to have the same set of goals. The main point is that these petty bourgeois nationalists, most of whom are opposed to communism, are objectively conduits of U.S. influence in Africa. This is what Henry Winston, National Chairman of the Communist Party, U.S.A., had to say about this new strategy: " . . . the role of Pan-Africanism within U.S. African strategy is to aid in penetrating African countries as they gain political independence, and to influence them to reject policies and leadership internally – and support externally from the socialist countries – that would help them choose and begin to advance along the non-capitalist path of development."[3]

When speaking of the theoretical errors Nkrumah committed while in exile on the question of how best to conduct the struggle for national and social liberation, it should be noted that in his last works he drew some concrete conclusions that made a definite contribution to the development of theory and practice with regard to the revolutionary process in Africa.

Some of his proposals, rejected earlier, are now being reconsidered and adopted in Africa. Thus, Nkrumah's idea of creating joint armed forces in order to bring about the final liquidation of colonialism and

---

[1] *Class Struggle in Africa*, p. 88.

[2] Stokely Carmichael, *Stokely Speaks . . .*, p. 186.

[3] Henry Winston, *Strategy for a Black Agenda*, International Publishers, New York, 1973, p. 25.

racism is being taken up with increasing frequency by the Organisation of African Unity as it faces the tasks presented by the liberation of the south of the continent and looks for ways of defending independent African countries against the threat of aggression. The idea of creating joint armed forces is supported by a number of political leaders such as Julius Nyerere, Kenneth Kaunda and Samora Machel. The OAU Liberation Committee has taken up the question of creating an African military command which would help "front-line states" resist armed attacks by the racist South.

Kwame Nkrumah was among the first in Africa to examine the cunningly disguised tactic by which splits in the national liberation movement are promoted. In his last works he revealed how imperialist circles support those African leaders and organizations who foment religious, cultural and tribal differences for the sake of attaining their own mercenary goals and oppose genuine freedom fighters.[1] One such organization he named is the Angolan National Liberation Front headed by Holden Roberto. Even then Nkrumah, in contrast to many African leaders, discerned the anti-popular nature of this movement.

In analyzing new trends in neocolonial policies Kwame Nkrumah gave particular attention to the phenomenon he called "collective imperialism" which he saw as being promoted by the European Economic Community, the International Monetary Fund, the World Bank and several other international organizations that are under imperialist control.[2] He realized that imperialism's ultimate goals are to safeguard the interests of transnational monopolies and to weaken the African countries' ties with the world socialist system. Nkrumah offered convincing proof that there is a link between neo-colonialism and the interests of the exploiters in African countries.

Today, when imperialism's ideological expansion in developing countries has reached unprecedented proportions and the U.S. has raised ideological sabotage to the status of government policy, Kwame Nkrumah's exposé of the mechanism by which this subversive work is carried out is extraordinarily relevant. "Psychological attacks," he explained, "are made through the agency of broadcasting stations like the BBC, Voice of Germany, and above all, Voice of America, which pursues its brainwashing mission through newsreels, interviews and other 'informative' pro-

---

[1]*Handbook of Revolutionary Warfare,* pp. 10-11.
[2]Ibid., pp. 5-7.

grammes at all hours of the day and night, on all wavelengths and in many languages, including 'special English'. The war of words is supplemented by written propaganda using a wide range of political devices such as embassy bulletins, pseudo-'revolutionary' publications, studies on 'nationalism' and on 'African socialism', the literature spread by the so-called independent and liberal publishers, 'cultural' and 'civic education' centres, and other imperialist subversive organizations."[1]

As a prominent member of the communist and working class movement, Rodney Arismendi, has noted, alongside the process of revolutionization there exist theoretical and political theses, generalizations and claims to exclusiveness. "If we separate the grain from the chaff," he points out, "we will gain a broader understanding of modern revolutionary practice while theory and practice with regard to revolution will be enriched."[2]

The evolution of Kwame Nkrumah's views on the revolutionary process in Africa is contradictory in nature. On the positive side, he recognized the existence of classes and class contradictions in African society, defined the driving forces behind the African revolution, realized that the process which results in the attainment of socialism is objective and law-governed, and recognized scientific socialism's universality. However, Nkrumah did not reach these conclusions by a "direct" route, nor by applying scientific methods to the study of the African revolution but rather through his interest in various types of "ultra-revolutionary" theories. That which Nkrumah learned about leftist radicalism broadened his political horizons somewhat. At the same time, however, it led to a number of incorrect conclusions concerning both the determination of the African revolution's tasks and the appropriate approach to some international problems. In addition, it kept him from completely mastering the only genuine theory of revolution – Marxism-Leninism. On the whole, though, Kwame Nkrumah's ideological evolution was progressive without question, for it led to his acceptance of several important tenets of scientific socialism.

Kwame Nkrumah did not get ready to return to Ghana merely by studying theoretical questions. He called on his supporters in Ghana to band together and create conspiratorial groups which would lay the ground-

---

[1]Ibid., p. 17.

[2]Rodney Arismendi, *Lénin, la revolución y América Latina,* Ediciones Pueblos Unidos, Montevideo, 1970, p. 441.

work for an action against the reactionary regime. "I would like everybody to organize in secret groups," he urged. "Organize in the villages and in the localities in the towns. Organize at your work places. Organize in your trade unions."[1] Proceeding from his new views on the methods of revolutionary struggle, Nkrumah thought that a small group of politically conscious patriots should begin an armed struggle. This center of resistance would then "grow" into a broad popular movement and a new, truly revolutionary party would be born. However, this organization functioned only in Nkrumah's imagination and in the reports of his messengers who mostly provided him with the news he wanted to hear.

Meanwhile, events in Ghana demonstrated that the new government was incapable of directing the country's development. Not only had the condition of the masses not improved but it continued to deteriorate. The military-political regime which had come to power as a result of the coup displayed total incompetency when it came to economic matters. Its leaders and the rank-and-file bureaucrats wallowed in corruption. The regime employed military-style methods in an attempt to eradicate the progressive gains the country had made and redirect it onto the path of capitalist development. There was no positive program – the regime's policies were simply the exact opposite of those the Nkrumah government had pursued. Class antagonisms in the country became sharply aggravated and found expression in a broad-based strike movement, even though industrial action was prohibited. Within the army itself sharp conflicts constantly arose between various groups of officers who wanted to grab a bigger piece of the pie. This forced those who supported the pro-Western orientation to "change the signboard."

The civilian government of Kofi Busia that came to power in September 1969 proclaimed that private enterprise would henceforth be unrestricted. The majority of state sector enterprises were turned into joint enterprises. Due to the weakness of the national bourgeoisie, foreign private interests became the government's partner in these. Ghana's already enormous foreign debt rose by one-quarter. The closing of a significant number of state enterprises and farms led to mass unemployment as well as a rise in the crime rate. A major devaluation of the national currency – the *cedi* – in December 1971 reduced the working people's standard of living. The *noveaux rich,* on the other hand, flaunted their wealth, acquired more often than not by illegal means. The policy of persecuting left-wing forces

---

[1]*Revolutionary Path,* p. 420.

which, although seriously weakened, continued to influence public opinion, remained in place.

In terms of foreign policy the Busia government was completely oriented towards the West. It was one of the initiators of the notorious "dialogue" with the racist South African regime, an act which was sharply criticized by the overwhelming majority of African states. In this period Ghana refused to actively support the African national liberation movement. All this led to the loss of the role it had once played in African and world affairs. Comparing the past and the present, Ghanaians began to recall Nkrumah and the years he had led the country more and more often. The government's unpopular domestic and foreign policies caused wide-scale displeasure among workers, peasants, students and trade unionists.

Following the military coup of January 13, 1972 led by Colonel Ignatius Acheampong, Kwame Nkrumah was given permission to return to his native land, the decision having been made in response to public pressure. However, he was unable to take advantage of this. By then he had already been suffering one year from a disease the true seriousness of which was known only to his personal physician and a very small number of the people around him. It was cancer. A decision was to send Nkrumah to Rumania for treatment.

In a Bucharest hospital, racked with pain but suffering more from the sense that he had not completed what he had set out to do, Kwame Nkrumah worked on his last book, *Revolutionary Path.* Into it went articles, speeches, excerpts from other works, and documents produced by organizations he had set up, all relating to his active political life. Each of the numerous chapters contained the author's comments, written from the perspective of the experience he had gained. Nkrumah wrote the conclusion on October 15, 1971.

On April 27, 1972 Kwame Nkrumah passed away. What had he thought about in that distant country? Undoubtedly about his mother, family and friends, about the joy of victory and the sorrow of defeat, about the incomparable tropical sun sinking on a sultry night into the cool depths of the ocean – about everything that the word *Africa* meant to him.

After Nkrumah's demise a three-day period of national mourning was declared in Guinea. In his native land state flags were lowered to half-mast. The question of where he was to be buried now arose. Before he left Guinea, Kwame Nkrumah had told the members of his family that he wanted to be buried in the village of his birth, Nkroful. In Ghana itself the public demanded that the body of the former President be brought back to his native land. Meanwhile, Nkrumah's old friend, Kojo Botsio, flew to Conakry with the remains. A. Sékou Touré turned down the many offers that were made by private Ghanian citizens to take responsibility for transporting the remains to Ghana. He announced that this would not occur until the Ghanian government provided an official guarantee that Nkrumah would be accorded the last honors as befitted him and that his former colleagues would be released from prison or given permission to return to Ghana.

The funeral was scheduled for May 16. On the eve a ceremony was held in the Palace of People in Conakry where the coffin containing Nkrumah's remains stood, draped with the Guinean flag. The heads of the delegations which had come to Guinea from forty countries offered their condolences to Fathia Nkrumah and her children. Much was said about the life and work of the deceased. A. Sékou Touré spoke. He concluded his eulogy with the words, "Nkrumah is not a Ghanaian, he is an African. Nkrumah will never die."[1] After the official ceremony Nkrumah's body was taken to the stadium where thousands of Guineans filed past the coffin in mournful silence, paying tribute to this loyal son of Africa. Then the interment took place.

Talks with the Ghanian government continued and at long last an agreement was reached. On July 9 Kojo Botsio and Fathia Nkrumah flew to Accra with the coffin containing Kwame Nkrumah's remains. On the following day it was taken to State House for the lying-in-state. The streets of the Ghanian capital were decorated in somber black and red. Radio stations played recordings of speeches made by the first Prime Minister and President of Ghana. His biography was read and public figures offered their recollections of him and pronouncements on his life and work. The line outside State House stretched for several kilometers. The Ghanaians had not forgotten their outstanding leader and during those days his name was on everyone's lips.

On the following Sunday, Nkrumah's remains were taken by helicopter to Nkroful. Nyanibah, old and nearly blind met her son and spent the entire night at his side. The other members of the village gathered near her home and kept vigil. The next morning the thousands of people who had come to pay their last respects watched as Kwame Nkrumah was lowered to his final resting place.

---

[1]Robin McKown, *Nkrumah. A Biography,* Doubleday & Company, Inc., New York, 1973, p. 165.

IX. CONCLUSION

Kwame Nkrumah's ideas, his political struggle and progressive undertakings had a big influence on Africa's history. He has gone down in history as an outstanding leader of the national liberation movement and an active fighter within the international front of anti-colonial and anti-imperialist forces.

An entire era is linked with Kwame Nkrumah's name, an era not just in Ghanian history but in the history of the whole African continent. This was the era of struggle for national liberation, the time when the independent African states took their first steps. Nkrumah was one of the most consistent fighters for Africa's liberation from colonialism. He created one of the first mass political parties in Africa to proclaim its goal to be the achievement of political independence – the Convention People's Party. The achievement of independence by Ghana in 1957, after a struggle to which Kwame Nkrumah made an enormous personal contribution, became an important revolutionary factor on the continent. For Africans, Nkrumah's name became a symbol of independence and the rebirth of their national dignity that had been degraded by colonialism.

To the end of his days Kwame Nkrumah was an indefatigable opponent of racism, colonialism and neo-colonialism. He ardently championed the idea of creating an anti-imperialist association to bring together the peoples and states of Africa and did a great deal to lay the foundations for such a union. The work he did in the name of furthering independent Africa's interests and strengthening the alliance of progressive forces within the national liberation movement received international recognition.

Nkrumah was the first statesman in Tropical Africa to lead his country along the path of independent development and he was the first to tackle the problems which the leaders of other African countries encountered later. He saw progressive socio-economic change as the key to resolving these problems.

Kwame Nkrumah is famous not just as a major political figure but also for his studies of the complex problems of the African revolution. The complete liquidation of colonialism on the African continent, the forms and methods of neo-colonialism and the prospects for Africa's economic and social development were all topics which came under his scrutiny. The historic service Kwame Nkrumah rendered, the primary product of his theoretical work and his political testament to coming generations of African revolutionaries is his recognition that the laws of class struggle are universal, his conviction that the problems facing independent governments can only be solved by applying the principles of scientific socialism, and his exposition of the fundamental elements which make up a revolutionary-democratic government's social base. One can only regret that Nkrumah came to these momentous conclusions, as R. A. Ulyanovsky so aptly put it, "enormously and tragically late"[1] and did not apply them in practice. They remained for him mere theoretical constructions. But Nkrumah reached this theory "the hard way": it was the result of both a painful reconsideration he was compelled to make of his own invalid theses and, to a certain extent, an analysis of the policies he pursued while in office and the methods he used to implement them.

Nkrumah's ideas and deeds continue to be of interest to Africans. This is, above all, explained by the fact that the goals for which he fought – the complete decolonialization of the continent, true political and economic liberation for the African states and Africa's socialist future – have not only retained their significance but have acquired greater relevance in conjunction with the continued expansion of the national liberation movement and the intensification of its social aspect. Many of Nkrumah's ideas concerning Africa's problems were ahead of their time and the prerequisites for their realization are only now being created. All this testifies to the fact that Nkrumah's ideological legacy is not a closed chapter in African political thought and that its positive aspects can and should be utilized today.

Kwame Nkrumah's ideas and experience continue to have an impact on the formation of African revolutionary-democratic ideology. The new generation of African revolutionaries is giving the experience of the first President of Ghana careful study. They add some of his concepts to their armory while critically reinterpreting others. Africa's socialist future and its unity, goals which Kwame Nkrumah ardently advocated, are two of the most important components of revolutionary democrats' ideological views.

[1] R. A. Ulyanovsky, *Politicheskie portrety . . . ,*

The multi-faceted work of Kwame Nkrumah contained errors, too. Most of them were completely understandable as they were the errors that came with theoretical and political growth. In many areas he trod an unknown path – not always the most direct one although he always had a clearly defined goal – a social system free of exploitation. Nkrumah's tragic greatness consists in the fact that his errors, many of which were unavoidable, formed a unique "political school," part of the extremely valuable experience the African revolution has gained and that revolutionary democrats in Africa today draw on as they proceed along the path of socialist orientation. That is why any assessment of Nkrumah's life and work must not be based on what he did not do or did not have time to do. As Lenin pointed out, "Historical services are not judged by the contributions historical personalities *did not make* in respect of modern requirements, but by *the new contributions they did make* as compared with their predecessors."[1] In this sense Nkrumah's accomplishments are considerable.

The significance of Kwame Nkrumah's work is also confirmed by the fact that many of the principles of domestic and foreign policy he applied enjoy growing popularity in Ghana today. And this is understandable. All of that country's most impressive economic, social and political achievements took place in the period when Ghana's first President governed. The events and processes which have occurred since 1966 have placed in sharp relief the superiority of the fundamental principles of socialist-oriented policies designed to promote the development of a young state. Time – the best and severest judge – makes it possible to separate that which is fundamental from that which is secondary, soberly to assess the successes and objectively to evaluate the errors and miscalculations made in the course of Ghana's non-capitalist development.

In the years since the proclamation of independence Ghana has traversed a difficult and contradictory path. It has perhaps tested more "models of development" and forms of government than any other state in Africa. Power has been held by revolutionary democrats and a military-political junta, by a pro-bourgeois civilian government and military regimes with poorly defined programs. At various times the principles of "African socialism," socialist orientation, capitalist development and even "ideological neutralism" have served as the basis for the country's socio-

---

[1]V. I. Lenin, "A Characterisation of Economic Romanticism", *Collected Works,* Vol. 2, 1973, pp. 185-186.

economic policy. Ghana's difficult recent history is, however, of no small importance to the African national liberation movement's theory and practice. Here, then, are the main lessons African revolutionaries have drawn from it.

Firm foundations for a socialist society can be laid only through systematic, scientifically based action directed toward the revolutionary transformation of all spheres of social life. Above all it is essential that effective political leadership be provided by the ruling party – bringing together the vital revolutionary forces of the country – politically conscious workers and peasants first and foremost. In its work the party should be guided by the principles of scientific socialism. This vanguard should become an efficacious tool for politically educating and organizing the masses. It should mobilize their creativity in the interests of further strengthening the progressive system, awaken in them genuine interest in revolutionary change and get working men and women more involved in running society's affairs.

In African countries, where the main modern classes are still in the process of being formed, the state and its machinery become a relatively independent force and play a key role in realizing economic and social programs and many other undertakings. That is why it is absolutely essential that states with a socialist orientation radically restructure the machinery of state during the initial stages of non-capitalist development. This should be followed by the liquidation of the old neocolonial machinery of state and the creation of a new type of machinery whose structure and methods of operation reflect the interests of the broad working masses.

One of the most important buttresses of any revolutionary-democratic government should be the army. In order to ensure that this is so, the military apparatus be restructured in such a way that the armed forces acquire and retain their revolutionary, popular character and consciously guard the revolution's gains. This is possible only if carried out under the direct control and supervision of the vanguard party. Only then can the armed forces of socialist-oriented countries become a major instrument of struggle for the creation of a new society, a tool for defending the revolution.

In order to advance along the path of socialist orientation, a country must pursue realistic economic policies, solidly based on science and aimed at mobilizing domestic resources more fully. Priority should be given to the development of the state sector – the material basis of popular power. At the same time, this must be combined with well thought out policies in regard to private domestic and foreign interests. These should play a role in the non-capitalist development of the country while under the effective control of its revolutionary-democratic government. Both the party and the people have a clear picture of the immediate and long-term goals of their country's economic development, of its pace and methods.

In the current era – the era of transition from capitalism to socialism – the socialist-oriented countries make their contribution to the development of the world revolutionary process and promote the triumph of the anti-imperialist struggle. That is why a major condition for the successful pursuit of socialist-oriented policies is the strengthening of political, economic and other types of cooperation between the countries that have opted for socialist orientation, on the one hand, and the USSR, the other countries where socialism is a reality, and the international communist and working class movement, on the other. These are their natural allies in the struggle for social progress, democracy and peace.

The socialist orientation is the main line of development for the newly free nations. It is a new path, still in the process of being laid out. It promises not only achievements but losses, too, brought on by the unavoidably intense struggle between the old and the new. The rejection, for whatever reason, of the socialist orientation in favor of capitalist development does not make it any easier for young states to accomplish the socio-economic tasks which face them. Rather, it aggravates old problems, creates new ones and sharply increases the country's degree of subjugation to neocolonialism.

The principles and ideas of the socialist orientation put down deep roots in the consciousness of the masses. In Ghana today these "recollections of the future" have become a major factor in the country's political life. It is possible to destroy by force the institutions of the socialist orientation – parties, the machinery of state, etc. – but the idea of progressive development itself cannot be destroyed, for the overwhelming majority of the population aspire to it and it is in their interests.

Notwithstanding the mixed character of Ghana's political forces, trends and slogans, in the final analysis the struggle is being waged between the supporters and opponents of non-capitalist development. The growing polarization of class forces extends and accelerates this process. This was clearly evidenced by the December 31, 1981 coup and the events that followed. A group of anti-imperialist servicemen led by Jerry Rawlings came to power.

The difficult times the country has experienced have left a deep mark on the consciousness of the Ghanian people, who stand firmly on the side of radical change, democracy and social progress. The patriotic forces of Ghana do not dissociate Nkrumah's name from their struggle to take a progressive path of development. To a certain extent they consider themselves his heirs although they are not afraid to point out his mistakes. Interest in the first President, his work and theoretical legacy is great, particularly among the young.

Kwame Nkrumah's life in politics was not a simple one. It contained dizzying rises, the happiness of knowing that he had helped make the country's vast achievements possible, an all-consuming passion for the work so important to the people of Ghana and Africa and the triumph of being the victor. It also contained shattering defeats, betrayal by his companions-in-arms, bitter loneliness and mistakes that had an effect not only on his own fate but on the fate of the entire country. But at all times, in every period of his life one idea possessed him – to free the African continent from every form of oppression. That is why Nkrumah has a permanent place in the minds of progressive people as a man who devoted his life to the selfless service of Africa and to the struggle for the social progress of its peoples and peace on Earth.

It will not be long before the human race enters the 21st century. The confrontation between the two chief social systems of this age is becoming ever more apparent. Capitalism is an obstacle to the further evolution of human society. Moreover, it represents a threat to the very existence of civilization on Earth. Socialism offers the only scientific prospect for development for all nations without exception. It is the guarantor that this planet will be cleansed of every remnant of colonial filth. It is the factor that preserves peace throughout the world. More and more people in different countries, on different continents are coming to this realization.

Books and Articles Cited

David Apter
1972   *Ghana in Transition,* Princeton University Press, Princeton, NJ

Rodney Arismendi
1970   *Lenin la revolución y América Latina,* Ediciones Pueblos Unidos, Montevideo

Kwesi Armah
1974   *Ghana: Nkrumah's Legacy,* Rex Collings, London

Dennis Austin
1964   *Politics in Ghana: 1946–1960,* Oxford University Press, London

1961   *Azia i Afrika Segodnya* (Asia and Africa Today), No. 11, Moscow

Timothy Bankhole
1963   *Kwame Nkrumah, His Rise to Power,* George Allen & Unwin, Ltd., London

Björn Beckman
1978   *Organizing the Farmers: Cocoa Politics and National Development in Ghana,* The Scandinavian Institute of African Studies, Uppsala

F. M. Bourret
1960   *Ghana—the Road to Independence, 1919–1957,* Oxford University Press, London

Stokely Carmichael
1971

Stokely Speaks: Black Power to Pan-Africanism, Vintage Books, New York

Basil Davidson
1973

Black Star: A View of the Life and Times of Kwame Nkrumah, Allen Lane, London

Regis Debray
1978

The Revolution on Trial. A Critique of Arms, Vol. 2, Penguin Books, Ltd., Harmonsworth

Franz Fanon
1968

The Wretched of the Earth, Grove Press, New York

Imanuel Geiss
1974

The Pan-African Movements, Africana Publishing Co., New York

Thomas A. Howell and
Jeffrey P. Rajasooria, eds.
1972

Ghana and Nkrumah, Facts on File, New York

Martin Luther King, Jr.
1967

Where Do We Go from Here: Chaos or Community? Harper & Row, New York

J. Ayo Langley, ed.
1979

Ideologies of Liberation in Black Africa, 1856–1870, Rex Collings, London

V. I. Lenin
1960 –

Collected Works, Vols. 1, 2, 3, 5, 9, 11, 21, 25, 27, 30; Progress Publishers, Moscow

Robin McKown
1973

Nkrumah. A Biography, Doubleday Company, Ic., New York

Jay Mallin, ed.
1969

"Che" Guevara on Revolution, A Documentary Overview, Univ. of Miami Press, Coral Gables, FL

Genoveva Marais
1972   *Kwame Nkrumah: As I Knew Him,* Janay Publish-
                                 ing Co., Chichester

Herbert Marcuse
1969   *An Essay on Liberation,* Beacon Press, Boston

Karl Marx and Frederick
Engels
1975 –   *Collected Works* (in 50 volumes), Progress Pub-
                                 lishers, Moscow; Lawrence & Wishart, Ltd., London;
                                 and International PUblishers, New York

Ali A. Mazuri
1967   *Towards a Pax Africana,* Weidenfeld and Nicolson,
                                 London

Y. E. Metcalfe, ed.
1964   *Great Britain and Ghana, Documents of Ghana
                                 History, 1807–1957,* Thomas Nelson & Sons, Ltd.,
                                 London

Jitendra Mohan
1967   "Nkrumah and Nkrumahism," in *The Socialist Reg-
                                 ister 1967,* Merlin Press, London

Kwame Nkrumah
1957   *GHANA: The Autobiography of Kwame
                                 Nkrumah,* Thomas Nelson & Sons, Edinburgh

1961   *I Speak of Freedom,* Heinemann, London

1962   *Towards Colonial Freedom: African in the Struggle
                                 Against World Imperialism,* Heinemann, London

1964   *Africa Must Unite,* Heinemann, London

1964   *Consciencism: Philosophy and Ideology for De-
                                 colonization and Development with Reference to
                                 the African Revolution,* Heinemann, Lond

1964   *Some Essential Features of Nkrumaism,* The Spark,
                                 Accra

1965   *Neo-Colonialism: The Last Stage of Imperialism,* International Publishers, New York

1968   *Dark Days in Ghana,* International Publishers, New York

1969   *Handbook of Revolutionary Warfare,* International Publishers, New York

1970   *Class Struggle in Africa,* International Publishers, New York

1973   *Revolutionary Path,* International Publishers, New York

Oginda Odinga
1967   *Not Yet Uhuru,* Heinemann, London

T. Peter Omari
1970   *Kwame Nkrumah, the Anatomy of an African Dictatorship,* C. Hurst & Co., London

George Padmore
1956   *Pan-Africanism or Communism? The Coming Struggle for Africa,* Dennis Dobson, London

Margery Perham
1951   "The British Problem in Africa," *Foreign Affairs, Voll. 29,* No. 4

G. V. Plekhanov
n.d.   "Force and Violence," *Works, Vol. 4,* Moscow

I. I. Potekhin
1959   *Gana Segodnya* (Ghana Today), Geografgiz, Moscow

W. Scott Thompson
1969   *Ghana's Foreign Policy 1957–1966. Diplomacy, Ideology, and the New State,* Princeton University Press, Princeton, NJ